with

SEXUAL HARASSMENT AND GENDER BIAS

Victoria Shaw, Ph.D.

THE ROSEN PUBLISHING GROUP, INC./NEW YORK

Published in 1998 by The Rosen Publishing Group, Inc.
29 East 21st Street, New York, NY 10010

Cover Photo by Christine Innamorato

First Edition

Library of Congress Cataloging-in-Publication Data

Shaw, Victoria.
    Coping with sexual harassment and gender bias / Victoria Shaw.
        p.   cm.
    Includes bibliographical references (p.   ) and index.
    Summary: Discusses sexual harassment, gender bias in schools and in
the workplace, laws against discrimination, the varying views of men and
women on this issue, and ways victims can find support.
    ISBN 0-8239-2547-1
    1. Sexual harassment—Juvenile literature. 2. Sexual harassment—Law
and legislation—Juvenile literature. 3. Sex discrimination against women—
Juvenile literature. 4. Sex discrimination against women—Law and legislation—Juvenile literature. 5. Sexism—Juvenile literature. [1. Sexual
harassment. 2. Sex discrimination against women. 3. Sexism.] I. Title.
HQ1237.S52 1998
305.3—dc21   98-23588
                                                                  CIP
                                                                  AC

Manufactured in the United States of America

About the Author

Victoria Shaw received her Ph.D. in psychology from Princeton University. She taught classes in child development at Teachers College of Columbia University and conducted research concerning adolescents. Shaw was awarded the James S. McDonnell Foundation Cognitive Studies for Educational Practice Post-Doctoral Fellowship. Shaw also participated in Big Brothers/Big Sisters and served as a social work intern in Connecticut.

Acknowledgments

I wish to thank my husband, Luc Faucheux, for his support and encouragement during the writing of this book and my daughter, Camille Faucheux, for being the inspiration for it. I also want to thank Patra McSharry Sevastiades, my editor, for her contributions to the text, and Yanne Menard for her able assistance. Finally, I wish to express my appreciation to Dr. Philip Johnson-Laird for his guidance, wisdom, and encouragement.

To Camille

Contents

Introduction 1

1 What Is Sexual Harassment? 6

2 Sexism and Gender Bias 13

3 Developing Gender Roles 23

4 Gender Bias at School 33

5 A Closer Look 50

6 Sex Discrimination on the Job 68

7 Sexual Harassment 87

8 Sexual Harassment, Gender Bias, and Men 102

9 What You Can Do 114

10 Finding and Giving Emotional Support 128

11 Fighting Back 135

Glossary 139

Where to Go for Help 140

For Further Reading 111

Index 145

Introduction

As soon as the bell rang Kenisha gathered her books from her desk and moved silently toward the door. She hoped to slip out of the room without attracting Mr. Moore's attention. This wasn't the first time that he had asked Kenisha to stay after class. Her grades in chemistry were not as good as last year's. Still, she was doing better than most of her friends. Science used to be one of Kenisha's favorite subjects. Now she dreaded going to chemistry class. She just didn't feel comfortable around Mr. Moore.

"Kenisha, I thought I asked you to stay after class," Mr. Moore called after her. Kenisha sighed, and walked back into the room.

Gayle Brown had noticed the change in her daughter's behavior over the past few months. Kenisha was quieter at home, and her grades at school were slipping. One day the principal at Kenisha's school called Gayle at work. Ms. Turner wanted to know why Kenisha had been absent from school that week. Gayle was livid. She couldn't believe that Kenisha had been skipping school. Gayle assured the principal that Kenisha would be in school tomorrow. The principal asked Gayle to stop by her office after school with Kenisha so they could discuss the problem.

When Gayle walked into the principal's office, she found Kenisha and Ms. Turner waiting for her. Ms. Turner motioned for Gayle to sit down in the chair next to Kenisha.

"I'm glad that you could make it, Ms. Brown," Ms. Turner said with a smile. "Shall we get started?" Gayle nodded. But Kenisha, who was staring down at her feet, didn't say anything.

"So, Kenisha, what's going on?" Ms. Turner asked. Kenisha just shrugged and kept staring at the floor. Gayle gave her daughter a disapproving glance. Ms. Turner sighed and continued, "I just don't understand. You've always been a good student. Why the sudden change?"

Kenisha reluctantly explained that her classes were "boring." Especially chemistry. She thought that things would be okay if she could quit her chemistry class. Ms. Turner looked displeased. She had seen too many girls at Kenisha's age start to lose interest in math and science.

"Tell me more about why you don't like your chemistry class."

"It's stupid, and . . . ." Kenisha hesitated.

"And?" Ms. Turner was determined to get to the bottom of this.

"I feel uncomfortable around Mr. Moore," Kenisha blurted out before she had a chance to think about what she was saying. Now she wondered whether she was going to be sorry.

"Look, honey," Gayle said with a sympathetic smile. "You don't have to be the best in every subject. Chemistry is difficult. Don't take it so personally."

"That's not it, Mom." Kenisha looked hurt and annoyed. She took a deep breath and continued, "Sometimes he says things, and he's always asking me to stay after class."

Kenisha told Ms. Turner and her mother how her teacher made comments about the way she looked and what she was wearing. Sometimes, when she had to leave for a game right after school, she would come to class in her basketball uniform. One time Mr. Moore told her she looked sexy in those "short shorts," and that she had nice legs. After that she always wore sweatpants over her shorts, no matter how hot the weather was. Another time when Mr. Moore asked her to stay after class he started asking personal questions about her boyfriend. These questions made her feel very nervous and uncomfortable. As she talked about these experiences, Kenisha started to cry.

"I feel really ashamed," she said as the tears streamed down her face. "This is so humiliating." Gayle leaned over toward Kenisha and rested her arm on her daughter's shoulder.

"Kenisha, you don't have to feel ashamed," Ms. Turner said. "You haven't done anything wrong." Ms. Turner leaned forward to see if she was getting through. "Kenisha, you've been a victim of sexual harassment."

At first Kenisha was confused. She had heard of sexual harassment. She had seen a program on television in which a teacher demanded that a student sleep

3

with him to get an A in his class. But Mr. Moore never asked for sexual favors. In fact, he never even touched her. Ms. Turner told Kenisha that sexual harassment is any unwanted or unwelcome sexual attention. When a teacher behaves in a sexual way toward a student he is taking advantage of his authority.

Ms. Turner gave Kenisha and Gayle some books to read about sexual harassment. Then she suggested that Kenisha schedule an appointment with the school psychologist. Ms. Turner explained, "Being a victim of sexual harassment can be confusing. The psychologist is a good person to talk to about it."

As Kenisha and her mother got up to leave, Ms. Turner said that she was proud of Kenisha for speaking up. "A lot of girls would be afraid to tell anyone that they were being harassed. You are a very courageous young woman."

About This Book

Kenisha was one of many women, young and old, who are victims of sexual harassment. Like many victims, Kenisha waited before coming forward. She was probably embarrassed and afraid that her teacher would retaliate. And Kenisha was not even sure that she had been a victim of harassment. Many people are uncertain what sexual harassment is, and what to do when they or someone they know is harassed. But sexual harassment is very widespread. In fact, at least one out of every two women will be a victim of sexual harassment at some point during her life. Sexual harassment is just one of the many forms of gender bias that are so common in our society.

This book tackles the problems of sexual harassment and gender bias and how they affect you. It discusses some common stereotypes about men and women and the difference between stereotypes and actual sex differences. It focuses on the problem of gender bias in school and the fact that many schools still discriminate against girls in the classroom and in athletics programs. The book also addresses issues of sex discrimination in the workplace and your legal rights, as well as sexual harassment and the laws that protect against it.

Since sexual harassment and gender bias involve and affect men, the book also explores the differences in how men and women view harassment.

The final two chapters explain what you can do if you, or someone you know, has been the victim of harassment and how victims can find emotional support.

What Is Sexual Harassment?

Kenisha was surprised to learn that she had been a victim of sexual harassment. Often harassment can be subtle, and sometimes victims are not sure what to call it. But sexual harassment is easy to define. To *harass* someone is to bother him or her repeatedly. *Sexual harassment* is bothering someone in a *sexual* way. Sexual harassment is defined as deliberate sexual behavior that is not asked for and not returned. It can be physical (such as touching someone in a sexual way), verbal (such as making unwelcome comments about someone's appearance), or nonverbal (such as flashing or mooning). Usually the harasser is someone in authority such as a teacher or a boss, but he or she may also be a peer or even a stranger.

In most cases, sexual harassment is against the law. The Equal Employment Opportunity Commission (EEOC), the federal office that enforces the laws against sexual harassment, gives the following definition of sexual harassment:

Unwelcome sexual advances, requests for sexual favors, or other verbal or physical conduct of a sexist nature constitutes sexual harassment when

(1) submission to such conduct is made either explicitly or implicitly a term or condition of an individual's

employment [*that is, a person must give in to the harasser in order to keep or be hired for a job*];

(2) submission or rejection of such conduct by an individual is used as the basis for employment decisions affecting such individual [*that is, a person must submit in order to get a promotion or other considerations on the job*]; or

(3) such conduct has the purpose or effect of unreasonably interfering with an individual's work performance or creating an intimidating, hostile, or offensive working environment [*that is, harassment occurs if the victim feels afraid of the person doing the harassing, feels anger or antagonism from the harasser, or is offended by the harasser's behavior*].

Sexual harassment is a form of sex discrimination, also known as gender bias. Gender bias occurs when an individual is denied opportunities, privileges, or rewards because of his or her sex. Examples of gender bias include refusing to hire a person for a job or excluding a student from a certain class on the basis of his or her sex. Unfortunately, sexual harassment, like other forms of discrimination and bias, is very common in our society.

Sexual Harassment in the News

In October 1991, Clarence Thomas was nominated U.S. Supreme Court Justice. There was little doubt that his nomination would be approved by the Senate Judiciary Committee. Then, two days before Thomas's nomination

was scheduled for Senate review, some startling information was revealed about his character. A law professor
at the University of Oklahoma, Anita Hill, accused
Clarence Thomas of sexual harassment. According to
Hill, she had been harassed by Thomas ten years earlier
when they worked together at the Equal Employment
Opportunity Commission (EEOC). She complained that
Thomas, her boss at the time, had regularly made sexual
comments to her and talked to her about pornographic
movies he had seen. Thomas's behavior had made Hill
feel very uncomfortable.

During the Columbus Day holiday weekend, millions of
Americans watched the Thomas confirmation hearings.
Hill made her case. Thomas firmly denied all of the
charges. It was her word against his. Then, in the closest
confirmation vote ever in Senate history concerning a
Supreme Court nominee, the committee approved
Thomas's nomination. Many experts on sexual harassment
were shocked and angered by the decision. They were
surprised that the politicians who judged the case knew so
little about sexual harassment. If there was any lesson to
be learned from the hearings, it was that there was a press-
ing need for education about sexual harassment. In fact,
before the trial many Americans had not even known that
sexual harassment was illegal.

Following the hearings, the issue of sexual harassment
became a topic of heated debate. At first, the majority of
Americans agreed with the Senate's decision. In a poll conducted by the *Wall Street Journal* and NBC News at the time
of the hearings, 24 percent of the people surveyed believed
Hill, and 40 percent believed Thomas. But as people

learned more about the issues many re-evaluated their beliefs. A year after the hearings, public opinion had reversed: 44 percent of the people surveyed now believed Hill, and only 34 percent still believed Thomas. Hill's bravery also inspired many women to fight back against sexual harassment. In 1992, a record number of women came forward with accusations of harassment. There was a 30 percent increase in sexual harassment suits filed from 1991 to 1992. Women came forward in fields such as government, business, and the military, where sexual harassment had been both common and largely ignored. In one highly publicized case, more than twenty female employees of Senator Robert Packwood filed charges against him for unwanted sexual advances. The senator was forced to resign.

During the same year as the Thomas hearings, Navy Lieutenant Paula Coughlin brought attention to the problem of sexual harassment in the military. Coughlin complained that she and twenty-five other women had been harassed by male naval aviators at that year's Tailhook Association convention in Las Vegas. According to Coughlin, hundreds of male aviators had lined a third-floor hallway of the Las Vegas Hilton and assaulted military women who were passing by. It took the Navy two years to investigate these complaints. It was soon clear that high-ranking officers, including the Chief of Naval Operations, Admiral Frank Kelso III, interfered with the investigation to cover up the scandal.

In the end, 140 cases of harassment were investigated, but no one was ever convicted. Still, the Tailhook scandal sent a clear message that such behavior would no longer be tolerated in the military. Admiral Kelso was forced to take early retirement.

The Facts About Sexual Harassment

The Thomas hearings and the Tailhook scandal called the nation's attention to what was already a widespread problem in American society. In a survey conducted by the *New York Times* in 1991, four out of every ten women polled said that they had been victims of sexual harassment.

Sexual harassment occurs in almost every profession and at every level, from secretary to corporate executive. And it is not limited to the workplace. It happens in schools, on the streets, and even at home. Although both men and women are sexually harassed, the majority of victims are women. The National Council for Research on Women (NCRW) estimates that 50 to 85 percent of American women will experience sexual harassment at some point during their academic or working life. Unfortunately, most harassment victims never come forward. They fear losing their jobs and their privacy. They feel humiliated, degraded, and helpless.

Before the Thomas hearings, and even today, many people believed that sexual harassment was harmless. But it is not. Sexual harassment is a form of gender bias. It singles out individuals for special treatment on the basis of their sex. Sexual harassment is part of a broader context of bias and discrimination against women. Harassment often occurs in the workplace, where men continue to hold most of the positions of authority. Each year thousands of harassed women quit, transfer, or are fired from their jobs. Sexual harassment is another way in which men can use their power to keep women "in their place."

Gender Bias

Gender bias refers to people's judging or behaving differently toward an individual because of his or her sex. The terms gender bias, gender discrimination, and sex discrimination are often used interchangeably. But the term "discrimination" also has a more specific, legal definition: Sex discrimination, or gender discrimination, refers to actions or policies that deny opportunities, privileges, or rewards to an individual because of his or her sex.

Many people believe that gender bias is a thing of the past. They believe that women and men have the same opportunities in our society. After all, women make up almost 46 percent of the American workforce, and this percentage is increasing. Women are doctors, lawyers, soldiers, pilots, and astronauts. Women hold powerful positions in business and government. The news media even declared 1992 the "Year of the Woman" because a record number of women were elected to Congress.

Unfortunately, although women have made progress, gender bias is still a serious problem. The average salary of a working woman is still two-thirds that of a working man. And although some women have managed to break into the traditionally male professions, the majority of working women are segregated into lower-status, lower-paying jobs, such as secretaries and nurses. Even after the so-called "Year of the Woman," women held only 6 percent of the seats in the Senate, and only 10 percent in the House of Representatives. People use the term "glass ceiling" to describe the invisible barrier that keeps qualified women from rising to the top of their fields. Today, the glass ceiling

11

is as strong as ever. Women make up less than 15 percent of the partners at the nation's largest law firms, 5 percent of surgeons, and only 3 percent of the top positions at the nation's largest companies.

The pattern of discrimination begins at school. Starting in elementary school, girls receive less time, attention, and encouragement from their teachers. Many girls learn to doubt to their own abilities. Studies show that girls tend to have lower self-confidence than boys, even when they receive better grades. Gender bias affects boys too. In school, boys are more likely be punished for bad behavior, be held back a grade, or to drop out of school. Whether you are male or female, the effects of gender bias can be devastating.

Sexism and Gender Bias

Julia was awakened from her daydreams by a loud knock on her bedroom door.

"Who is it?" she called out, although she knew by the knock that it was her younger brother, Robert. Robert cracked open the door and peeked in.

"Go away, I'm studying," Julia yelled.

Robert ignored his sister's order, pushed open the door, and made himself comfortable at the foot of the bed.

"What does it mean to be 'sexist'?" ten-year-old Robert blurted out. The question caught Julia completely off guard.

"What does it mean to be sexist?" Julia repeated the question. "Why do you want to know?"

Robert explained that one of the girls in his class, Molly, had said that he was sexist and that she didn't want to be his friend anymore. Robert was confused because he didn't know what the word meant. "This afternoon at recess, Molly wanted to play football with the boys," he explained. "We said 'no way.' Everybody knows that football isn't for girls."

"Well," Julia responded, "that sounds pretty sexist to me too." Robert still looked confused. Julia continued, "A sexist is someone who treats males and

females differently based on stereotypes about the two sexes, like 'Girls don't play football.'"

"But none of the other girls in my class ever wanted to play before," Robert protested.

"Maybe that's because the other girls in your class are sexist too. Lots of people believe in stereotypes like 'Sports are only for boys,' or 'Playing with dolls is only for girls.'"

"But girls aren't tough enough to play football," Robert retorted. "Molly might have gotten hurt."

"That's another stereotype, that girls are weaker and more fragile than boys," Julia laughed. "But I can think of some very tough women. The gymnast Kerri Strug was tough when she vaulted with a broken ankle in the 1996 Olympics. And what about all of the great female triathletes."

"Hm, I never thought about it like that before."

What Is Sexism?

Sexism is one way of thinking about the sexes. It is a form of discrimination or bias. Another term for sexism is gender bias. Gender bias is usually easy to recognize. When Robert and his friends excluded Molly from their football game, they were biased against her because she was a girl. The boys were biased against Molly because of their ideas about what behaviors, or *gender roles*, are suitable for boys and girls, and they believed that Molly was stepping outside of hers.

Gender roles are the behaviors that society teaches us are "correct" for boys and girls, respectively. Gender roles influence and can limit women and men. Like Robert, many people believe that girls who play aggressive sports like football and boys who sew are behaving "inappropriately," because they are not staying within their gender roles.

Gender roles are based on gender stereotypes. These are assumptions made about the characteristics of each gender, such as physical appearance, physical abilities, attitudes, interests, personality traits, or occupations. People use these stereotypes to make judgments and predictions about individuals based on their sex. People apply stereotypes without even realizing it. Consider the following riddle:

A patient is admitted to the hospital emergency room. The surgeon sees the patient and says, "Oh, no—that's my son." The nurse asks the surgeon, "Would you like me to call his father?"

Who is the surgeon?

Of course, the surgeon must be the patient's mother. The riddle is a riddle only because, according to stereotypes, most physicians, especially surgeons, are men.

There are many stereotypes about men and women. Which sex is more cooperative? Which is more competitive? Most people would agree that females are more cooperative and males more competitive. In fact, most people generally agree about the stereotypical characteristics of males and females. Women are typically viewed as being nurturing, gentle, emotional, passive, and dependent. Men are typically viewed as being ambitious, aggressive, active, and independent. Men are "supposed" to act in the world and make things happen. Women are "supposed" to be concerned with relationships and emotions.

The Difference Between Sex and Gender

If you're like most people you probably didn't know that there was a difference between *sex* and *gender.* In everyday language these two terms are used almost interchangeably. But there is an important difference: Sex usually refers to biological differences; gender usually refers to our cultural ideas about masculinity and femininity.

When we talk about gender roles, we are talking about the roles that society tells us are correct for men and women. They are based on gender stereotypes, or *cultural ideas* about the differences between males and females. Gender roles have "should's" in them: Boys should fix cars, not dinner; girls should fix dinner, not cars. But in fact, both boys and girls can learn to fix cars and dinner.

Sex roles, on the other hand, are based on the *biological* differences between males and females. They do not involve "should's." For instance, it is a biological fact that only women are able to bear and breast-feed children, whether they choose to or not.

Sex roles are the same for all cultures. But gender roles can differ from culture to culture.

Among the Maya people of South America, weaving cloth is considered women's work, and mothers pass the tradition on to their daughters. But among the Mande-speaking peoples of Western Sudan, weaving cloth is considered men's work, and fathers pass the tradition on to their sons. Clearly, both men and women can weave. But in each society, gender roles determine who is allowed to do what.

Sadly, even young children often agree with these stereotypes. In one study involving a group of eleven-year-olds, more than 90 percent agreed that the adjectives *weak, emotional, gentle, talkative, fickle,* and *mild* probably described a girl, and the adjectives *strong, aggressive, independent, adventurous, ambitious,* and *dominant* probably described a boy. As you may already have noticed, the stereotypically male traits seem more valuable and important than the female traits. Unfortunately, this also reflects a general bias in our society: Males are viewed more positively than females.

Sexism is so common in our society that even the most open-minded people probably believe at least some of these stereotypes. But some people are more prone to believe them than others. Research shows that men are more likely to believe gender stereotypes than women. Men also feel more pressure to live up to these stereotypes. Since male traits and behaviors are more highly valued by society, it is easier for women to act "like men" than for men to act "like women."

But individuals pay a price for clinging too tightly to gender stereotypes. Research shows that women who show "more stereotypically female traits" suffer from high anxiety and have low self-esteem. They also receive less approval from their peers. And men who adhere to gender roles usually have difficulty expressing emotion. This may cause them to mask powerful emotions by turning to drug or alcohol abuse or to develop ulcers or other medical conditions.

As it turns out, the individuals who are most success-ful and well adjusted tend to exhibit both male and female traits. This may be surprising. Our society is so caught up in gender stereotypes that *androgyny* tends to get a bad rap. Androgyny is the combination of stereo-typically male and female traits within one individual. Many people think that androgyny has to do with physical appearance and people's looking not distinctly male or female. But androgyny is about behavior, not appearance.

Androgynous individuals are those who show a com-bination of male and female traits and behaviors under different circumstances. For example, a woman who is nurturing when she is at home with her children may be tough and aggressive enough to fight fires, jump out of planes, or climb the corporate ladder. Androgynous indi-viduals do not allow themselves to be limited by gender stereotypes. They feel more free to engage in traditional-ly "masculine" or "feminine" behaviors regardless of their gender.

Sex Differences: Fact or Fiction?

There's no denying that males and females are different. The most obvious differences are physical. On average, males and females differ in strength and size. Men tend to be taller and have more upper body strength than women. But those are just averages. They do not tell us anything about individual men and women.

In the 1979 New York Marathon, Bill Rodgers was the first man to finish the race. About sixteen minutes later, the first woman to finish the race, Grete Waitz, crossed the finish line. The last male runner finished about five hours later.

This demonstrates two ideas. First, while male runners are faster than female runners on average, you can't predict how any individual runner will finish based his or her sex alone. Second, the difference in the performance level within the sexes (Bill Rodgers vs. the last male runner) was much greater than the difference in the performance level between the sexes (Bill Rodgers vs. Grete Waitz).

Physical differences between the sexes are one thing, but what about differences in behavior and personality? You may wonder if the stereotypes are true. Are boys really more assertive, ambitious, and logical? Are girls really more nurturing, social, and emotional? When it comes to behavior and personality, the sex differences are not as big as you might think. In fact, many of the stereotypical differences between men and women do not exist at all.

In the 1970s Eleanor Maccoby and Carol Jacklin, psychologists at Stanford University, reviewed more than 1,500 scientific studies to sort through the stereotypes and find the facts. They studied hundreds of behaviors that were supposed to be the result of sex differences. In the end, they found only four actual differences between males and females, and the differences were small:

(1) Males are more aggressive than females. From birth onward boys are more aggressive, both physically and verbally, than girls.

(2) Girls have better verbal skills than boys. From about age ten onward, girls score better than boys on standardized tests of verbal skills such as punctuation, spelling, vocabulary, and reading comprehension. Girls are also better at using language to express their thoughts and ideas.

(3) Boys have better visual-spatial ability. On average, boys are better at doing things like reading maps. This may account for the stereotype that boys have a better sense of direction.

(4) Boys have better mathematical ability. From about age thirteen onward, boys outscore girls on standardized tests of mathematical ability.

It is important to keep in mind that these differences are small. It is also important to note that the differences within the sexes are much greater than the differences between them. Most important, *these differences reflect group averages that may or may not apply to any particular individual.* Many individuals within each group do not fit the pattern. In other words, you cannot predict traits like aggressiveness, mathematical skills, or verbal abilities of an individual simply by knowing his or her sex.

Why Are There Sex Differences?

What causes these differences? There are different theories. Some theories attribute the differences to "nature," or biological factors. For example, some people believe that sex differences in mathematical, spatial, and verbal abilities are caused by differences in the male and female brain. Other theories attribute sex differences to "nurture," the way people learn different behaviors as a result of growing up male or female. This research is still controversial.

It is unlikely that either biological or social factors alone are responsible for sex differences. For instance, animal research has shown that the level of the male sex hormone testosterone in the brain is related to aggressive behavior. The more of this hormone an animal has, the more aggressive it is. But research has also shown that animals secrete higher levels of testosterone when they are in situations in which it becomes necessary to behave aggressively. As a result, it is difficult to tell whether the hormones cause the behavior or the behavior causes the hormone levels to rise. It is probably a little of both.

Most researchers, including Maccoby and Jacklin, believe that sex differences have a lot to do with the ways boys and girls are raised. Children get information about sex-role stereotypes from many different sources, including parents, teachers, and peers. They find sex stereotypes at home and in school. These stereotypes are reinforced by the toys they play with, the clothes they wear, and the shows they watch on television. All of the

influences affect children's judgments about other people, but they also affect how they view themselves. As
children learn that boys and girls are supposed to behave
in certain ways, they adopt those behaviors themselves.

Developing Gender Roles

From the moment they are born, girls and boys are treated differently. Boys are dressed in blue and girls are dressed in pink. Boys are viewed as bigger, firmer, and stronger, while girls are viewed as sweeter, softer, and finer. People are also rougher with baby boys than with girls, and they speak in a softer, higher-pitched voice to girls than to boys. Studies show that people act differently around the same baby depending on whether they think it is a boy or a girl. In fact, many people do not even know how to react to a baby if they don't know its sex.

Throughout childhood, parents hold different expectations for their sons and daughters. Generally speaking, sons are expected to be more active and daughters more emotional. Boys are encouraged to be aggressive, and they are discouraged from expressing their feelings. Girls, on the other hand, are encouraged to be expressive and are discouraged from being aggressive. Parents expect males to be more independent and less "fragile" than females. Male children are less restricted and are allowed more freedom to explore the environment.

Parents tend to discourage their children from behaviors and activities that are supposed to be for the other sex. For example, girls may be discouraged from playing sports, and boys may be discouraged from playing with dolls. This is especially true for boys. The same parent who wouldn't think twice about buying a baseball glove for his or her daughter may hesitate before buying a doll for his or her son. As we discussed earlier, the sex stereotypes for males are more rigid than those for females. It is considered "worse" for a boy to be a "like a girl" than for a girl to be a "tomboy."

Children also learn a lot about gender stereotypes through observation. They watch their mother cleaning the house and their father and brother playing catch in the backyard. They notice when their sister is praised for cooking dinner, but their brother is teased for taking an interest in cooking. From these sorts of observations, children make conclusions about how they should and should not behave on account of their gender. Psychologists refer to this learning process as modeling. Children model themselves after important people in their lives like parents, teachers, siblings, and peers.

Children are not passive observers. As they develop, children look for structure in their lives and are driven by an internal need to fit into this structure. They observe the world and try to develop sets of rules that they can apply to a wide variety of situations. A child's knowledge of his or her own gender and its implications is known as *gender identity*. As children acquire gender identities, they also acquire stereotypical ideas about what it means to be a boy or a girl.

Around the age of two years, children learn some of the stereotypical characteristics of boys and girls. They start to notice that boys and girls look different and behave in different ways. Interestingly, children at this age do not understand that there are fixed anatomical differences between boys and girls. Instead, they believe that you can change a boy into a girl by cutting his hair and dressing him in girl's clothing.

Young children work very hard to make themselves fit the social definitions of their gender identity. Girls may insist on wearing pink. Boys may avoid playing with dolls. Girls prefer playing with other girls, and boys with other boys. Young children cling to these rigid stereotypes even without the encouragement of parents or other significant role models. It seems that they are internally driven to fit with their newly acquired concepts of gender identity. Fortunately, as children mature they generally learn to be less rigid in their views about the sexes.

Young children also expect other people to behave in stereotypical ways. In fact, children in preschool tend to take these sex-role stereotypes much more seriously than adults. You probably remember at least one child in your kindergarten class whom all the kids teased. Maybe the kids called one of the boys a "sissy" because he wanted to play with dolls instead of toy fire trucks. Or maybe they teased one of the girls because she was aggressive and liked to play ball with the boys. At a very early age, children learn from other children that it is more acceptable to behave according to sex-role stereotypes.

The Power of the Media

Julia couldn't help thinking about her brother's sexist behavior. She wondered how a ten-year-old had

*already learned to believe in so many sex-role stereo-
types. Julia knew that her parents had always tried to
raise her and her brother in unbiased ways. Robert
always helped with the housework, and Julia helped
her mother fix things around the house. When Julia
was little, her parents bought her toy trucks and
signed her up for Little League. She couldn't understand how Robert could have learned to be so sexist.*

*Julia couldn't concentrate on her homework, so she
decided to go downstairs and watch some television
until dinnertime. She found Robert curled up on the liv-
ing room couch, watching a cartoon program. Julia
walked over to the set and reached out to change the
channel.*

*"Hey, I'm watching that," Robert protested. "That's
not fair! I was here first!"*

*"Okay," Julia decided to give in. "But I hope the
show's almost over." Feeling exasperated, she sat down
on the couch next to her brother and picked up a mag-
azine from the coffee table. The sound from the television was so loud that Julia couldn't help but half listen
to the program. As she understood it, the plot involved
a group of super-hero dinosaurs who were fighting to
rescue a cavegirl from the clutches of vicious, meat-eat-
ing dinosaurs. She listened as the "good" dinosaurs
threatened the "bad" dinosaurs in their deep male voic-
es, and the little cavegirl cried for help.*

*Suddenly, Julia had a very good idea of how her
brother had learned to be so sexist. Television was full of
sex stereotypes and biases—especially the cartoons that
he spent so much time watching. Julia decided that it
was time to have another talk with her younger brother.*

Stereotypes in the Media

No matter where you look, you're going to find sex-role stereotypes. The media are no exception; television programs, movies, magazines, and music videos all perpetuate the stereotypes. Television is probably the most significant source. On average, American children spend almost thirty hours a week watching television. The average child has watched 18,000 hours of television by the time he or she has graduated from high school. In fact, the average child spends more time watching television than in school! Television has a large effect on how children and adults view the world around them. Unfortunately, television portrays a world that is full of sexism and sex-role stereotypes.

Women still play a limited role in the television world, although that seems to be changing somewhat. Think of your favorite television shows. Who are the main characters? How many of them are women? As you probably discovered, most of the characters on television are men. In fact, there are three times as many male characters on television as female characters.

Now, think about the roles that women do play. Female actresses often play the supporting roles in television— even on shows that are recognized as promoting positive values for children, such as *Sesame Street,* where the familiar characters are overwhelmingly male. This seems to indicate a widespread belief among television producers that female characters will not attract as much interest as male characters. Unfortunately, they are unwittingly reinforcing this sexist belief. The good news is that women are increasingly being cast as central characters.

Television is full of stereotypes about the sexes. Even when playing central characters, women are usually seen as nurturing, weak, and passive. Men are seen as ambitious, powerful, and aggressive. Women are more likely to be portrayed as the victims of crime, whereas men are more likely to be the criminals. Women on television are often seen only as "sex objects." If you think about your favorite shows, you'll probably discover that the majority of women are young, thin, and attractive. Children and teenagers are portrayed less frequently than adults on television, but when they are it is often in sex-stereotyped ways. Boys are more active and aggressive than girls. Girls are more likely to help with the housework. Boys are more likely to play sports.

The majority of characters on television still follow traditional divisions of labor. Most women on television are married, and most of these married women do not work outside the home. When working women are portrayed, the plot often focuses on domestic or romantic dilemmas rather than on their careers.

Television also gives a biased view of the career choices available to men and women. Men on television usually work in high-profile, high-paying professions such as physicians and lawyers. Women usually work in traditional female occupations such as secretaries, nurses, waitresses, and teachers. Fortunately, some new shows feature women who work in high-profile professions. But even in shows in which the main characters are strong women the majority of female characters on the show are still portrayed in stereotypical ways.

Sex stereotyping on television is even worse in programs targeted at children, like Saturday morning cartoons and after-school programming. Male characters outnumber female characters nearly five to one in these children's programs, and characters are almost always presented in stereotypical ways. Male characters are more likely to use aggressive behavior to solve problems. Female characters are more likely to be portrayed as weak and passive. Fortunately, this too seems to be changing gradually, with more independent, problem-solving female characters showing up.

Commercials for children are extremely sex stereotyped. Ads for toy cars, trucks, and action figures always feature boys, whereas ads for dolls always feature girls. When an advertised product is supposed to be for both boys and girls, the ads usually feature only boys.

Sex stereotypes are also common in programs for teenagers. Music videos are notorious for conveying biased images of both sexes. In music videos women are often portrayed as being submissive, passive, physically attractive, and sexual. Women are often used as decorative objects. Many music videos openly degrade women. Males in videos are often portrayed as aggressive and dominant, and sometimes as gang members and thugs.

Fortunately, not everything on television reinforces gender stereotypes. There are a few new shows that explore the complexities of the working lives and personal lives of strong, interesting women. Several popular shows currently feature strong female characters. *Xena: Warrior Princess* features a warrior who fights injustice using both her wits and physical force; Kathryn Janeway is the captain in *Star Trek: Voyager*; *The Secret World of Alex Mack* concerns a bright teenage girl with superhuman powers; and *Where in the World Is Carmen San*

Diego?, another children's show, focuses on a woman who is a clever mastermind.

You may be able to think of other examples of programs in which women play important roles. But one of the reasons it is easy to think of these programs is that they are still relatively rare. Also, even as more of the major networks add shows that feature strong, independent women, the smaller networks and cable stations show reruns of old television programs and movies that convey outdated and misleading ideas about the sexes. Popular "classics" such as *Bewitched* and *I Love Lucy* reinforce the idea that women should stay at home and not "meddle" in men's work. Frequently, these syndicated shows are on in the morning or after school, when children and some teenagers tend to watch television.

Images on television affect the way people view themselves and the world around them. Significantly, studies show that children who watch a lot of television tend to be more sexist than children who spend their free time in other activities such as reading. In one study, children who watched a lot of television were more likely to agree with the sexist statements "Women are happiest at home raising children" and "Men are born with more ambition than women."

Children who watch television also hold more stereotyped ideas about which occupations are suitable for males and females. When researchers asked preschool boys who watched a lot of television what careers they would choose if they were girls, the boys couldn't think of any. The girls, on the other hand, didn't have any difficulty thinking of careers that they would choose if they were boys. This suggests that television teaches young children that boys have more career opportunities than do girls.

This is just one of the many ways television teaches girls that they are not as important as boys. Not surprisingly, studies have shown that girls who watch a lot of television have more negative attitudes about their own sex.

It Can Go Both Ways

The next day when Julia came home from school, she found Robert and some of his friends playing tag in the front yard.

As Julia was walking her bicycle into the garage, she heard a loud screech. She turned around and saw Robert sitting on the lawn screaming something at one of the other boys. Julia didn't recognize the other boy, but she immediately noticed that he was much bigger than her brother.

"Why did you do that?" Robert screamed. "You didn't have to tag me so hard." Robert's face was bright red, and he looked as if he were on the verge of tears.

"Oh, poor little Robbie," the other boy said in a mocking tone. "Did I hurt you?"

Robert didn't answer. He seemed to be using all of his energy to keep from crying.

"Look, Robbie's going to cry," another boy said, and then he started to laugh. Robert bit down hard on his lip. He looked ashamed.

"Robert, you are such a wimp," the first boy continued. "I don't even know why we play with you." Then he turned around and walked away, and the other boys

31

followed. As they were leaving, they kept shouting at Robert and calling him names like "baby" and "girl."

Julia was shocked. She couldn't believe that the boys could be so mean. She couldn't believe that they were so hung up on sex-role stereotypes. By the time Julia reached Robert, he was sobbing.

"Don't let those creeps get to you," Julia said as she knelt down beside her brother and tried to comfort him. But when Julia put her arm on Robert's shoulder, he pulled away.

"Don't touch me," he screamed. Then he wiped the tears from his face and started to get up. "I'm not a baby!"

Julia didn't know what to say. She wished that her brother would let her try to comfort him. She wanted to tell him that he wasn't a wimp, and that it was okay for him to cry. She wanted him to know that he didn't have to pretend to be so tough. For the first time, Julia realized that sexism is hard on boys too.

The Cost of Gender Stereotypes

As Julia discovered, both males and females suffer as a result of sexism and gender stereotypes. Stereotypes limit the choices that boys and girls have about what they want to do and who they want to be. Sexism, or gender bias, prevents individuals from exploring the activities and interests that are best suited to their personality and abilities. It needlessly keeps an individual from reaching his or her full potential.

Gender Bias at School

4

For a moment the crowd was silent. Everyone was holding their breath, just waiting to see if the shot was good. Then the ball swooshed through the net and the crowd went wild. Everyone was yelling, and hugging, and jumping up and down. It was a close game, but they had done it. The Westbrook Wildcats were the new regional champs, and they were on their way to the state tournament.

"We did it!" Selena yelled at the top of her lungs. She could hardly contain her excitement. None of the players could. This was the first year in Westbrook High School's history that the girls' basketball team had earned a place at the state championship tournament. It had been a tough year, but they had some really talented players, and everyone on the team had worked hard. From here on they felt that nothing could stop them.

But the next day when the team showed up for practice, the coach broke the bad news.

"I know how hard you girls have worked this season," the coach explained, "but there just isn't enough money in the budget to take the girls' team to the state tournament. Maybe next year."

For a moment the gym was silent. It was as if the words didn't even register. Then Jessica, who played forward, and Jenny, who played guard, turned and stormed out of the room. Some of the other girls followed. But Selena stayed behind. She couldn't just swallow her anger like the other girls. She had dreamed of going to the state tournament since her first year on the team. Now she was a senior. Next year she'd be going to a college where they didn't even have a girls' basketball team. For her, this was the last chance.

"Coach, that just isn't fair," Selena said, trying to keep calm. "We worked hard all year so we could go to this tournament."

"I know how you feel," the coach responded in a sympathetic voice, "but it's out of my control. Things are really tight this year. We just don't have enough money in the budget."

"But the boys' team is going to the tournament," Selena protested. "They go every year. Why not ask them to stay home from the tournament this year?"

The coach looked surprised. It had never occurred to him to ask the boys' team to stay home from the tournament. The boys' basketball team, after all, was the pride of the school. They hadn't missed the tournament once in the past ten years. How could he break a ten-year tradition? He tried to explain this to Selena, but she didn't seem to understand.

"Ten years ago, this school didn't even have a girls' basketball team."

Selena exclaimed, "Tradition is no excuse for sex discrimination!"

"Sex discrimination?" the coach asked in a doubtful tone.

"Yes. This is sex discrimination," Selena replied. "And I'm going to fight it."

Gender Bias in Athletics Programs

Recently, there has been a lot of controversy about sex discrimination in school athletics programs. Although a great deal of progress has been made in the past few decades, males and females still do not receive equal treatment when it comes to high school and college athletics. A 1992 report by the American Association of University Women (AAUW) found that 70 percent of the public school districts in the United States did not provide girls and boys with equal opportunities. Nearly twice as many high school boys participate in team sports as girls, and schools spend more money on boys' athletics programs. A look at our nation's colleges and universities shows a similar picture. Women make up roughly one third of all college athletes. In addition, women athletes receive less than 24 percent of college sports operating budgets, 30 percent of athletic scholarship money, and less than 18 percent of the money used to recruit new athletes.

Part of the problem is that people do not take female athletes seriously. Most people still believe in the cultural stereotype that only boys are supposed to be good at athletics. A 1990 study of secondary schools in Michigan found that students considered nearly all sports to be male domains. The only exceptions were figure skating, gymnastics, jump rope, and cheerleading. Moreover, when girls in this study were asked, "How would your life be different if you were a boy?" many said that they would be

35

more likely to play and enjoy sports. The bias against girls in sports starts early in life. Beginning in preschool, boys are expected to be more active and aggressive and are therefore encouraged to participate in contact sports and other athletic activities. In fact, boys who do not enjoy or excel in athletics are often looked down upon by peers and adults. Girls are simply not expected to enjoy or succeed at these physical activities. As a result, girls develop less self-confidence in their athletic abilities and are less likely to participate in athletics.

When it comes to athletics, girls lack role models. Until very recently, opportunities for female professional athletes were mostly limited to stereotypically "female" sports, such as gymnastics and ice skating.

Fortunately, it looks as if this might be changing. In 1997 the first women's professional basketball association, the Women's National Basketball Association (WNBA), was established. And in the 1997–98 season women became referees for the National Basketball Association (NBA), the National Hockey League (NHL), the National Football League (NFL), and Major League Baseball. These accomplishments were met with some resistance, but the WNBA and the women referees have proven their abilities and their staying power.

Girls lose a lot by not participating in sports. Exercise is an important part of a healthy lifestyle. Girls who begin to participate in sports in high school lower their risk for developing breast cancer by 40 to 60 percent. Playing sports also reduces the risk of developing osteoporosis and heart disease, and improves a girl's self-esteem. Girls who play high school sports are more likely to describe themselves as "highly popular" than nonathletes. These girls also have higher grades than their nonathletic peers and are three times more likely to graduate from high school. Female high school athletes are 80 percent less likely to have an unwanted pregnancy and 92 percent less likely to abuse drugs. Finally, participating in sports helps students to develop leadership skills. High school athletes are more likely to aspire to be leaders in their communities.

Beyond Athletics

Athletics programs are just one of the many areas in which girls and boys receive unequal, and often unfair, treatment in school. In the corridors and in the classrooms, boys and girls tend to have very different experiences. In a study conducted by the Michigan Department of Education, students were asked: "Are there any policies, practices, including the behavior of teachers in classrooms, that have the effect of treating students differently based on their sex?" One hundred percent of the middle school and 82 percent of the high school students surveyed answered yes. This unequal treatment has negative effects on both male and female students.

Girls tend to lose out when it comes to academics. As students progress through school, girls' achievement test scores decline while boys' scores increase. Girls are more likely to go to college and get better grades in school, but scholarships based on standardized test scores are twice as likely to go to boys. As we will discuss in chapter 5, boys are better prepared in math and sciences and thus tend to score higher on tests that measure math and science achievement. But sex differences in test performance exist even when girls and boys have similar abilities. As a result, many experts believe that standardized tests may be biased against girls.

Sex discrimination is also common in vocational classes. Originally, vocational education was intended only for boys. The goal was to provide work skills to high school boys who were not going to college. Later, when vocational classes were added for women, the curriculum mainly focused on preparing them to become wives and mothers. Many vocational classes were segregated by sex. Schools required girls to take classes in "home economics" and boys to take classes in industrial arts, shop, and mechanics. Boys were trained for careers in industry and business, while girls were trained for lower-status clerical jobs. The idea was that girls would be working only for a few years until they were married.

Although schools are no longer allowed to "track" students on the basis of their sex, sex segregation in vocational programs is still a problem. The majority of female students still train for traditionally female fields, which have lesser status and are lower paying than traditionally male fields. A 1992 study by the National Coalition for Women and Girls in Education found that women make up 70 percent of students training for health-related fields like nursing, and 77 percent of students studying occupational home economics. Men make up 77 percent of the students training for trade and industry jobs, and 72 percent of those in technical education. In addition, some high school teachers and counselors still push girls toward more traditional careers.

Sex discrimination in education does not happen only to students. In primary and secondary school, women make up the majority of teachers and the minority of high-level administrators. According to a 1991 report by the U.S. Department of Education, women make up only 30 percent of all public school principals. In colleges and universities, men are professors, department chairs, and administrators, while the majority of women are assistant professors and instructors. This sort of sex discrimination also affects female students, who lack role models of powerful women. From their earliest school experiences girls learn that the people with the most authority are men.

Taking Up the Challenge

When Selena made it back to the locker room, some of the other girls were still hanging around complaining about the coach's decision.

"It's so unfair!" Jenny Woo complained. "We worked hard all season, and for what?"

"So we could stay home while the boys' team goes to the tournament," Selena answered in a sarcastic tone. "I thought males and females were supposed to get equal treatment in school."

Sally Walters agreed. "And this is just the tip of the iceberg. Now that I think about it, the boys' team has been getting better treatment all along."

"What do you mean?" Jenny asked.

"Well," Sally continued, "the boys' team gets to practice right after school, while we have to wait three hours until their practice is finished. "

"That bugs me too," Selena agreed. *"By the time I get home from practice every night I barely have time eat dinner and finish my homework before I collapse into bed."*

"Right, and when it comes to the games, the guys' teams get all the prime-time slots again. When's the last time the girls' team got to play a Friday night home game?" Sally asked.

"You know, my mother hasn't been able to see us play once this whole year," Selena complained. *"They always schedule our games early in the evening when she's still at work. The boys' varsity and J.V. teams get all of the later time slots."*

"And what about our uniforms?" Sally added in frustration. *"Last year the boys' team got brand-new uniforms for free. We had to buy ours."*

"I thought the parents' booster club paid for their uniforms," Jenny interrupted.

"It's still unfair," Sally said. *"I mean, when's the last time the booster club raised any money for any of the girls' teams?"*

"And besides," Selena added, *"if the booster club earned extra money for the boys' teams, then there should be more money left in the school's budget for the girls' team."*

"And it's not just the boys' basketball team," Sally said. She was so excited that she was almost shouting. *"Other sports are the same way."*

"You're right," Selena agreed, *"like the boys' baseball team gets the good field, while the girls' team has to practice on the elementary school's field three miles away."*

Jenny said, "You guys are right, the school has def-
initely been discriminating against female athletes."
"There's got to be something that we can do about it,"
Selena chimed in.

"Aren't there laws to protect against sex discrimi-
nation in school?" Jenny asked. Nobody answered.

"I'm sure that the law is on our side," Selena said.
"It must be. We've just got to find out more so that we
can make our case to Principal Turner."

Laws Against Discrimination at School

One of the reasons that sex discrimination in school is still
so common is because students do not know their rights.
But the laws against sex discrimination guarantee the right
to fair treatment in school as well as the right to fair treatment at work.

Sex discrimination in education is not a new problem.
In colonial America it was considered dangerous to edu-
cate women beyond the elementary level. The idea was
that too much education might lure women away from
their proper place as wives and mothers. As a result,
women and girls were excluded from public and private
schools and colleges. The few existing schools for
women were limited to teaching domestic skills such as
cooking, sewing, and child care. Even when schools
became coeducational, most had different curricula for
male and female students. Girls were required to take
classes in cooking and housekeeping, whereas boys took
classes in auto mechanics. In fact, less than twenty-five
years ago schools still openly discriminated against

41

female students when it came to careers, vocational education, counseling, academic programs, and athletics. They also discriminated against students who were single mothers or were pregnant.

Title IX

In 1972, Congress enacted Title IX of the Educational Amendments of 1972. The goal was to put an end to the long history of sex discrimination in our nation's schools. Title IX states, "No person in the United States shall, on the basis of sex, be excluded from participation in, be denied the benefits of, or be subjected to discrimination under any education program or activity receiving federal funding." This law makes it illegal to treat males and females differently or separately. The law applies to any educational institution that receives federal funding. This includes all public schools, from preschool through college. Private colleges and universities are also covered by Title IX because they receive federal funding through financial aid programs. Title IX is enforced by the Office of Civil Rights (OCR) of the U.S. Department of Education. If a school is found to violate Title IX, the OCR can withdraw its federal funding.

Title IX and Athletics

In the case of high school and college athletics programs, Title IX requires that physical education classes be coeducational. There are only two cases in which boys and girls can be separated: When boys and girls differ in ability (in which case girls must be allowed to try out for boys teams, but not vice versa); and in contact sports such as basketball and wrestling. In these cases the law requires separate but equal treatment of girls and boys. Title IX applies to all aspects of men's and women's athletics programs. For instance, the law requires that male and female athletes receive equal amounts of athletic financial assistance. The law also requires that boys' and girls' teams be provided with similar equipment and supplies, and that they have similarly equipped locker rooms and practice and playing facilities. The law even applies to how much money teams are given for travel expenses.

To determine whether males and females are receiving equal treatment, the OCR compares the entire men's athletics program with the entire women's program, rather than comparing the men's and women's teams in each sport. All teams and programs are included in this comparison. It does not matter whether a sport generates its own revenue or receives outside donations. Men's sports programs usually have a longer history and tend to earn more money than women's sports. But the history and tradition are not excuses for discrimination.

Title IX also requires that the selection of sports offered and the level of competition offered by schools "effectively accommodate the students' interests and abilities." The OCR uses three tests to determine whether a school is in compliance with this aspect of Title IX. The first test compares the ratio of male and female students at the school with the ratio of male and female athletes. Thus, if 50 percent of the student body is female, then females should also make up approximately 50 percent of the athletes. This is sometimes referred to as the "proportionality test," because it requires schools to have proportional representation of women athletes. If members of one sex are underrepresented among athletes, there are still two other tests to determine if the school is discriminating against women.

To pass the second test, the school must be able to show that it has a history of expanding opportunities for women and is continuing to increase its programs to meet the demands of female athletes. For example, the school may be in the process of adding new teams for female athletes, such as creating a basketball program, or it may be developing programs to recruit more female athletes.

If the school cannot show that it is trying to expand opportunities for women, the third test requires it to prove that its present program already meets women's interests.

Does Title IX Work?

Ideally, Title IX should mean that male and female athletes are given exactly the same opportunities and resources. Unfortunately, there is room for different interpretations of what it means to have "equal opportunities." For instance, the law does not require that schools spend the same amount of money on boys' and girls' teams. Instead, it requires that both teams be given necessary funds. However, it is left up to school administrators to determine how much funding is "necessary." As a result, schools sometimes get away with spending less money on women's athletics programs.

Another problem is that Title IX is not always enforced. The OCR rarely investigates schools unless they receive a complaint. Unfortunately, few people complain. Like Selena and her friends, many students are not familiar with the law and do not know enough about their rights. Others are afraid of how they will be treated if they come forward. Also, it is hard to be sure whether or not a school is violating Title IX without getting full information about men's and women's sports programs.

Recent federal legislation should help solve this problem. In 1994, Congress passed the Equity in Athletics Disclosure Act, which requires colleges and universities to make public important information about men's and women's athletics. For example, schools must disclose exactly how much money they spend on men's and women's sports, how many men and women participate in sports, and even the number of male and female coaches employed by the university.

This law, which went into effect in 1996, should help ensure that schools comply with Title IX.

Controversy

The following week at lunch, Selena and Sally were surprised to get the cold shoulder from some of their friends. When they sat down at their usual table, Mark and Brent grabbed their lunch trays and started to get up.

"Hey, where are you guys going?" Selena asked.

"For some reason, seeing you two makes us lose our appetites," Mark said.

"That was really rude," Sally said. "What's the problem?"

"I'll tell you what the problem is," said Brent. "Thanks to you girls, the coach told us that the school is going to have to drop the wrestling team next year."

"What do you mean, drop the team?" Sally asked. "They're not going to have wrestling anymore?" Brent nodded.

"How come?" Selena asked.

"Because they're going to spend our money on the girls' teams," Mark said, frowning.

"Wow," Sally said. "I never thought that the school would get money for the girls' teams by cutting other teams."

"It's not fair," Brent said. "You guys get more money, and we lose our team."

"Maybe there's a way to keep the wrestling team and other boys' teams and still fund the girls' teams," said Selena.

"I know," said Mark. "Why don't they just cut the budget of the boys' basketball team? They have a lot of money, and it seems only fair that the rest of us get an equal share."

"Hey, wait a minute," Gerald broke in. He was sitting at the end of the table. "We earn that money. People pay to come see us play."

"Hey, we'd earn money, too, if we were scheduled to play Friday night home games," Selena said.

"Or if we had cheerleaders, a pep band, and the money to hand out programs at every game," Sally added.

"Does your team really earn enough money to pay for all of that?" Selena asked.

Gerald wasn't sure how much money the boys' team earned, or if they even made a profit. He had assumed that the boys' team earned what they got. "I don't know," he said. "I think so."

Unfair Practices

In April 1991, Brown University announced that it would demote the women's gymnastics and volleyball teams, along with two men's teams, from varsity to club status because of budget problems. The administration explained that the teams could continue to exist as "club sports" but would have to raise their own money for uniforms, travel, coaches, and other expenses. The female athletes were outraged. They believed that the university already provided too few athletic opportunities for women. They argued that by dropping the women's teams, Brown was discriminating against its female students, and was therefore violating Title IX. One year later the two women's teams filed a class-action lawsuit against the university.

Although Brown had one of the nation's best records for providing athletic opportunities to female students, the courts found that Brown still failed to provide equal opportunities for male and female students. While men were only 51 percent of the student population at Brown, they made up 61 percent of the athletes. The court ruled in favor of the female athletes.

Following the Brown case, between 1992 and 1995 twenty-nine other schools were sued for similar Title IX violations. The courts found all of these schools guilty of sex discrimination.

Dividing the Pie

The Brown case called the nation's attention to the problem of sex discrimination in college athletics. The case has also prompted universities across the country to eliminate discriminatory practices on their own campuses to avoid being sued for violating Title IX. Unfortunately, in order to make room in the budgets for women's sports, many schools cut low-profile men's sports like gymnastics and wrestling, rather than take money from the budgets of the more expensive, higher-profile teams like football. As a result, some people believe that Title IX sometimes causes reverse discrimination because it increases opportunities for women while decreasing opportunities for men. But Title IX was not intended to eliminate men's sports. The goal was to give women the same opportunities that men have had all along. Title IX requires only that men and women have equal opportunities. The truth is that as more women have entered high school and college athletics, men's participation in sports has increased, not decreased.

Supporters of Title IX blame the high-profile sports such as men's football and basketball for using up the majority of schools' athletic budgets. Football, in particular, has received a lot of criticism. Many high schools and colleges spend up to 50 percent of their budgets on men's football. The rest of the money has to be divided between other men's and women's teams. Since there is no women's equivalent of football, the only way to comply with Title IX is to cut down on the money spent on other men's sports. Rather than cut their budgets, these teams blame female athletes for taking money away from the men's sports. To justify themselves, football and basketball coaches often claim that their sports make money and therefore deserve a larger share of the budgets. But the truth is that only a few of the top college teams earn enough money to support themselves, let alone to return any money to the university. The vast majority of high school and college football and basketball teams actually lose money.

The controversy over Title IX and athletics programs is far from over. Although Title IX has been around for more than twenty years, sex discrimination in the nation's schools has not been entirely eliminated. Sports is just one of many areas in which males and females receive unequal treatment in schools.

A Closer Look

5

Rayna slammed her fist against the table. Everyone, including the study hall monitor, turned to look as she slumped back into her chair.

"I've had it with this stuff," Rayna whispered loudly in frustration. "Math is impossible!"

"Come on, Rayna," Lucas said. "You're great in math. You're in the advanced class, and you're getting A's. You'll figure it out."

Rayna shook her head. She had been working on the same problem for twenty minutes and she wasn't getting anywhere. Yesterday's homework had been the same way. If she was so smart, then why were these problems so difficult for her?

"I don't know," Rayna sighed.

Rachel, who was sitting across from Lucas, whispered, "Hey, Rayna, I've heard that scientists have discovered that girls' brains are not made to do math. It's in their genes."

"That's ridiculous," Lucas retorted.

"So explain why more boys take advanced math classes, and why most of the great mathematicians are men," Rachel said. "Males are just better at math than females."

Lucas rolled his eyes. "The reason that there are not more girls in advanced math classes is because girls aren't encouraged to do well in math the way boys are."

"You know," Rayna said quietly to Lucas, "there are only two girls in my Advanced Algebra class."

"Rayna, you know it's not because girls can't do math. That's just a stereotype. You love math," Lucas said.

"I know," Rayna said. "Sometimes I feel embarrassed that I enjoy it so much. People think I'm weird. I swear, my older sister thinks I'm some kind of math mutant. And she says no one ever dates girls who are brains."

"Not true," Lucas said.

Just then Henry, a boy from Rayna's math class, tapped her on the shoulder. "Rayna, have you gotten anywhere with your math homework? I'm still stuck on the first problem."

"No, I'm stuck too," Rayna said. "You want to work on it together?"

Sex Differences in Academic Achievement

You may believe that boys are better than girls at math and science, and girls are better than boys at reading and writing. But are those stereotypes really true? During the past two decades a lot of research has been done on sex differences in academic abilities. The results of this research have been mixed.

When children start school, girls do better than boys in almost all academic areas. Girls learn to read earlier. They are better at spelling and writing. Girls are even better at math.

As girls and boys progress in school, things change. Girls continue to do better at reading and writing. But, by the time they reach middle school, boys start to do better than girls at math. As we discussed in chapter 2, high school and middle school boys score better than girls on standardized tests of mathematics abilities. There are twice as many boys as girls in the most advanced math classes. And boys are more likely to pursue careers that involve mathematics, such as engineering and accounting.

Sex differences in the sciences are even more striking. From the early school years through college, males do better than females on almost all measures of achievement in science. Boys do better on standardized tests, they get better grades in school, and they even win more awards in science fairs and other science competitions. Male students show the greatest advances in physics, chemistry, and earth and space sciences. But sex differences show up in all fields of science. What is worse, the size of this "gender gap" is increasing.

Is It Biology?

What causes these sex differences? You might assume, like Rachel, that these differences are the result of biology. After all, males and females are biologically different. They have different chromosomes, different anatomy, and different sex hormones. It seems reasonable that sex differences could be caused by these biological differences. And over the years, many experts have argued that sex differences in mathematics ability had a biological basis; according to one theory, boys' brains were better equipped to do math.

As it turns out, there is little evidence that biology accounts for much, if any, of the differences between males' and females' mathematical abilities.

First of all, these sex differences have always been very small. The small differences that do exist are limited to the very best students; there are no sex differences between boys and girls with low or moderate mathematics ability. Sex differences in mathematics ability do not appear until early adolescence. Before that time, girls actually show a slight superiority to boys.

Second, if there were biologically based differences between the sexes, we would expect them to occur at all ages and all levels of ability. And they do not.

Finally, the most convincing evidence against a purely biological explanation for the gender gap is that over the past ten years sex differences in mathematics have been decreasing. If these sex differences were the result of biology there is no way that they could change in such a short period of time.

Expectations Affect Performance

Today, most experts agree that sex differences in academic achievement have more to do with gender role stereotypes than biology. At a very young age children learn that math and science are for boys. Boys learn that they should do well at math and science. Girls learn that they can't do well. Parents, teachers, and peers all play a significant role in conveying these gender-stereotyped messages. Studies show that parents have different expectations for their sons and their daughters. Starting in kindergarten, parents expect their daughters to do well in reading and their sons to do well in math. These expectations are shaped by the stereotypes. In one study, researchers questioned parents of junior high school girls and boys about their children's mathematical abilities. There were no actual differences in the abilities of male and female students. But the parents told a different story. Parents of girls believed that their children were less talented in mathematics than did the parents of boys. Parents of girls also believed that their children had to work harder to succeed.

The result of these stereotypes is that girls lag behind boys not only in actual achievement, but also in self-confidence and willingness to take advanced courses. Research shows that as girls move from childhood to early adolescence they have less and less confidence in their ability to do math. Around the time that students start middle school, girls, but not boys, show a sharp drop in confidence in their ability to do math. This is the same age at which sex differences in mathematics achievement first begin to appear.

In a classic study, psychologists Elizabeth Fennema and Julia Sherman found that these declines in girl's self-esteem appear *before* the decline in their actual performance. In other words, middle school girls begin to believe that they are not good at math, and so they stop doing well at math. The stereotypes seem to have a greater effect on girls' self-esteem than does their actual ability. Even girls who are highly successful in mathematics and science tend to have less self-esteem than equally high-achieving boys.

Boys and girls have different views about how important math and science are to their lives. Although training in math and science is very important for both sexes, boys tend to think it is more important than girls do. High school girls, even those who are enrolled in advanced math and science classes, are much less likely to choose math and science-related careers than boys. A study of high school seniors in Rhode Island found that 64 percent of the boys who had taken physics and calculus, but only 18.6 percent of the girls, were planning to major in science or engineering in college.

Recall Rayna's complaint that her sister called her a "math mutant" because she is good at math. This highlights another reason why girls shy away from mathematics and other advanced courses: peer pressure. Girls not only believe that they are not supposed to enjoy or be good at mathematics, but they expect their peers to act the same way.

Some girls also believe that boys are intimidated by girls who are smart. These girls get the idea that they can either be smart and strive for intellectual achievement or they can be accepted by their peers, but not both. The sad consequence is that some girls try to play down their intelligence so that they will "fit in." Unfortunately, these girls wind up cutting themselves off from important career opportunities in the future. By opting out of advanced mathematics courses in high school, girls eliminate more than half of the possible college majors. Often those majors are the kind that lead to jobs in the most prestigious and highest-paying fields. Society also loses out when girls are discouraged from achieving their full potential.

The Formal Curriculum

Rayna couldn't wait to tell Lucas what she had discovered in math class. She found him on the way to the lunch room.

"Hey, Lucas, wait up!" Rayna shouted after her friend. "I have something to show you."

They found a table in one corner of the lunchroom. As Lucas opened his lunch bag Rayna started to share her news. "Remember our discussion this morning in study hall?" Rayna asked. "We were trying to figure out why some girls don't do well at math?" Lucas nodded. "Well, I think I've discovered one of the reasons."

Rayna took out her algebra textbook and opened it on the table in front of Lucas. "Look at this problem set," Rayna said pointing to a list of story problems.

"So?" Lucas said.

"So, all of these stories are about men!"

Lucas pulled the book closer and started to read through the problems.

"Look at this one," Rayna said, pointing to the first problem, "it's about four boys traveling to a soccer match. And the next one is about two boys trying to build a train set. Here's another, with a male repairman needing to fix refrigerators. "

"Here's an example with a girl in it," Lucas said, pointing to one of the problems.

"That's the only one!" Rayna exclaimed. "There are seven problems. And she's purchasing flowers."

"I see what you mean," Lucas said. "It's mostly about guys."

56

"They're also full of stereotypes," Rayna said. "Boys play sports and build things, and girls buy flowers."

"What about our other schoolbooks? Do you think that they could be sexist?"

"I don't know," Rayna replied. "But I'd sure like to find out."

What Rayna and Lucas discovered is a problem that has been worrying educators for the past twenty years. From math and science textbooks to children's storybooks, to films, many of the instructional materials used in the classroom are full of gender-role stereotypes and biases. These materials are an important part of the schools' "formal curriculum," the course of study prescribed by the educational community and followed by so many educators.

In fact, about 90 percent of class time involves use of instructional materials such as textbooks and workbooks, library books, and films. Although these materials are intended to provide information about math, science, reading, and writing, they may also convey messages about the roles of males and females in society, as well as in the classroom.

Identifying Sexism in Classroom Materials

In 1975 a group called Women on Words and Images published the ground-breaking report, *Dick and Jane as Victims: Sex Stereotyping in Children's Readers.* The researchers analyzed the stories that elementary school students use when they are learning to read. They looked at factors such as the sex of the characters and how the

57

male and female characters were portrayed. What they discovered was shocking. Girls in these stories were portrayed as passive, weak, and fearful. They were concerned about their looks and about not getting dirty. Boys, on the other hand, were heroic, strong, and clever. They were in control of their emotions and their environments. Mothers in elementary school readers were always at home cooking, cleaning, and sewing. When fathers came home from work they played catch with their sons and told their daughters that they looked pretty.

The results of the "Dick and Jane" study opened the eyes of the educational community to the problem of sexism in the formal curriculum. Researchers across the country began looking for sex biases in everything from science textbooks to foreign-language materials. In almost every study, researchers found that women were rarely represented at all in these materials. And when women were portrayed, it was in sex-stereotyped ways.

Gender-Biased Subject Matter

Sexism in the formal curriculum is not limited to the way information is presented; it also affects what information is taught in the first place. For the most part, women's interests and achievements in the formal curriculum are not taken seriously. Think back to what you studied last semester. Did you learn about any important women? Chances are you can count on one hand the number of women about whom you've studied.

In history class, you probably learned a lot about the male war heroes and generals. What did you learn about women? You rarely find women in history books. And

58

when women are presented they usually play limited, stereotypical roles. For instance, all history books talk about Betsy Ross, the woman who sewed the American flag. But the rest of the discussion of the American Revolution focuses on men.

Many educators have pointed out that history really is *his*tory because it mostly focuses on men. Everyone learns about wars. But women did not fight in wars. Did you ever wonder what the women were doing while the men were fighting? From reading most history textbooks, you get the impression that women never did anything interesting or important. Most textbooks ignore the important roles that women have played in history. And most school history classes do not even discuss the history of the women's rights movement.

History is not the only part of the curriculum from which women are frequently missing. Think about the books you studied last year in English class. You might have read stories by John Steinbeck and Nathaniel Hawthorne, and plays by William Shakespeare and Arthur Miller. But how many female authors did you study? Probably not too many. For the most part, the "classics" in literature were written by men. Historically, female writers were not taken seriously in the world of literature. If you want to study the contributions that women have made to society you probably have to wait until college. There you can take special "women's studies" courses that teach about the contributions that women have made in art, history, literature, and science.

Unfortunately, a lot of girls are receiving the message through the formal curriculum that women never do anything important. Sex bias in the curriculum can affect the way students view themselves and the world around them. Girls using biased materials learn that most of the really important things that have been done in history have been done by men. Studies have shown that the use of unbiased instructional materials improves girls' academic self-esteem and achievement.

Luckily, the situation is slowly starting to change. Some school districts and state departments of education have demanded unbiased educational materials. Some publishers of school textbooks have issued guidelines for producing unbiased textbooks and other instructional materials. Of course, that does not mean that all schools will buy the books. Many schools cannot afford to upgrade their textbooks. Other teachers may prefer to keep the old textbooks rather than revise their lesson plans. Still, it is a step in the right direction.

The Hidden Curriculum

What students learn in school is not limited to the formal curriculum. Students also learn from their experiences inside and outside the classroom. This kind of learning is sometimes referred to as the "hidden curriculum" because it is not what teachers intend to teach. Unfortunately, this hidden curriculum contains many lessons on sex-role stereotypes. Through their interaction with their teachers and with other students, girls and boys receive very different messages about who they are, how they should behave, and what they are capable of achieving.

During the past twenty years many studies have looked at the way teachers interact with their students. In nearly every case researchers have found that male students receive more attention from teachers than female students.

Starting in preschool classrooms, boys get more hugs and more help with their work than girls. This pattern continues though elementary school to high school, and even in college, where teachers are more likely to call on male students than female students. The effect of these differences in attention is that, on average, from preschool through college a girl receives 18,000 fewer hours of teacher attention than a boy!

One reason why boys receive more attention may be because they ask for it. A study conducted by researchers David and Myra Sadker found that elementary and middle-school boys called out the answers eight times more often that their female classmates. And teachers often encourage these differences in behavior. In the Sadkers' study, when boys called out the answers their teachers listened to what they had to say, but when girls called out the answers the teachers usually responded with comments like, "Please raise your hand if you want to speak."

Boys get more attention even when they do not demand it. Teachers are more likely to call on boys even when they do not volunteer answers. As girls move through the grades they have less to say. By the time students reach college, men are twice as likely to make comments in class as women.

Studies have also found differences in the kinds of attention girls and boys receive. For instance, teachers tend to give boys more valuable and specific feedback on their work. Studies show that teachers give boys more detailed instructions about how to solve problems and complete tasks. With girls, teachers are more likely to do the task for them. In this way, boys get the message that they are capable and that they can do tasks on their own. Girls, on the other hand, get the message that they are dependent on their teachers to get things done.

As early as elementary school, girls receive less praise from their teachers than boys. When girls do get praise it is more likely to be for good behavior than for academic performance.

When it comes to negative feedback, boys tend to be reprimanded for poor behavior, whereas girls tend to receive negative feedback for poor academic performance. In fact, while less than one-third of the negative feedback given to boys is based on academic performance, two-thirds of the negative feedback that girls receive is for poor performance. In this way, teachers send different messages to their male and female students. Boys learn that they are smart, even though they are not very well behaved. Girls learn that they are not very smart but that teachers will like them if they sit quietly, write neatly, and follow instructions.

Teachers do not necessarily show preference to boys on purpose. Their behavior has been shaped by gender-role stereotypes. The stereotypes are usually unconscious, and teachers are probably not even aware that they have them. Many teachers, however, are aware of the problems caused by gender-role stereotypes and make special efforts to teach in unbiased ways.

Unfortunately, studies show that even teachers who try to be unbiased sometimes unknowingly teach according to gender-role stereotypes.

According to stereotypes, boys do not take school as seriously and do not work as hard as girls. These assumptions affect the way teachers treat their male and female students.

When female students do well on a report or a problem set, the teacher usually rewards them for "working so hard." When girls don't do well, many teachers assume that they've given it their best shot. In other words, they figure that if a girl fails, it is because she lacks the ability to succeed.

On the other hand, no matter how well a boy does, teachers usually assume that if he tried harder he would do better. When boys do fail, teachers generally assume that they didn't try hard enough and encourage them to try again.

Teachers pass on these stereotypes to their students. When girls succeed in school, they believe it is because they worked hard. When they fail, they believe it is because they lack the ability to succeed. If a girl believes she lacks the ability to succeed, she is more likely to give up.

When boys succeed, they attribute their success to their ability. When they fail, they tend to attribute it to lack of effort. As a result, boys are more likely to believe that they have control over whether they succeed in school.

School often teaches girls to be passive and cautious. Girls who are rewarded only when they do well are less likely to take risks; many girls avoid academic challenges because they are afraid to fail. Owing largely to socialization, in the elementary school classroom the former describes the boys and the latter describes the girls.

The hidden curriculum does not only affect girls' academic achievements, but it can also affect ideas about their self-worth. As girls progress through school, they have less and less confidence in themselves and their abilities. A nationwide survey conducted by the AAUW in 1990 found that, on average, 69 percent of elementary school boys and 60 percent of elementary school girls could say of themselves "I am happy the way I am." The same survey found that among high school students 46 percent of boys and only 29 percent of girls agreed with that statement. Apparently, the hidden curriculum further teaches girls that they are less valuable than boys.

Pressures on Boys

Lucas sat next to Rayna on the bus ride home. "You know, I guess I'm a little jealous of you," Lucas admitted to Rayna. "You're so much better at math than I am."

Rayna was stunned. Lucas was one of the most talented people she knew. He had won awards for his short stories and his artwork. She never expected him to be jealous of her.

"What's there to be jealous about?" Rayna asked. "You're an amazing artist, and I'd give anything to be half as good as you are at creative writing."

"Yeah, I guess I'm okay at those things, but I feel like a total loser because I'm stuck in the remedial math class. Last year my parents were so worried that they had me tested to see if I had a learning disability."

"What happened?" Rayna asked.

"The psychologist couldn't find anything wrong with me. She told me that I just have to try harder. You know, I almost wish they had found something wrong with me. Then I'd have an excuse for not doing well in math."

Rayna wondered why Lucas thought that he needed an excuse. She knew some of the girls in Lucas' math class, and none of them seemed to worry the way he did. It occurred to Rayna that boys must feel a lot of pressure to do well in traditionally male disciplines like math and science.

Masculinity and Education

Boys, like girls, suffer when they try to fit into rigid sex-role stereotypes. Boys are expected to excel in mathematics and athletics. They are expected to be tough, aggressive, independent, and unemotional. But how many boys can you think of who actually live up to all of these traditional standards? Many boys, like Lucas, do not fit the stereotypes. And even for boys who do, the pressure to maintain the status of "best and brightest" can be overwhelming.

Boys enter kindergarten at a slight disadvantage. They have already been through five years of male socialization, which has taught them to be independent, active, and aggressive. As we have seen, such training has many positive aspects. But this kind of behavior is not as well tolerated in school, where students are expected to sit quietly and play cooperatively rather than aggressively. In fact, owing to gender-role stereotypes, most teachers expect their male students to misbehave in class and are more likely to reprimand boys than girls for bad behavior. As a result, some boys learn to think of themselves as "troublemakers."

Many teachers also believe that boys are more intelligent than girls. As a result, they tend to put more pressure on boys to be successful academically. This can benefit many boys. But when a boy does not live up to these expectations, teachers may think that there is something wrong with him. This helps to explain why boys who have academic difficulties are more likely to be labeled as learning disabled or to be held back a grade than are girls.

Whether they succeed or fail, boys still feel pressure to live up to society's expectations. But unlike most girls, boys are taught to avoid expressing their emotions. This can be dangerous; when a person tries to hide his or her feelings in the face of overwhelming pressures, those feeling may be expressed in an unhealthy way. Some researchers think this is why a greater proportion of boys than girls commit suicide and abuse alcohol and drugs.

When it comes to gender bias in school, both boys and girls lose out. Girls learn to have less self-confidence in their academic abilities, especially when it comes to math and science, and may give up easily because they feel that they lack control over their ability to succeed or fail. Or they may not fulfill their potential in traditionally "male" subjects because they want to fit in. Boys are expected to succeed in certain fields, especially math and science, and feel a great deal of pressure to do so. Unfortunately, many boys have difficulty coping with these pressures since they have been raised to mask their emotions. Gender biases in school are harmful to everyone involved.

Sex Discrimination on the Job

Carmen stormed out of the ice cream parlor, relieved to see her friends Amanda and Jung, who were waiting for her.

"Yo, Carmen. What's up?" Jung asked.

"I just found out that Justin makes $5.50 an hour, while Pam and I only make $4.00 for the same job. And it's not like he works any harder than we do. In fact, Pam and I are always getting stuck with the crappy jobs like cleaning out the freezer while Justin gets to work the cash register. And Justin hardly ever has to work on Saturday nights. He comes into the shop with his girlfriend, and they hang around eating ice cream for free while we're working."

"That really stinks," Amanda exclaimed. "Did you talk to the owner?"

"Yeah, that's the worst part. He said that he knows we all work hard, but Justin is a boy."

"What does that have to do with it?" Amanda asked.

"That's exactly what I said," Carmen replied. "But Mr. Roberts seems to think that boys need more money than girls. He said that boys have more expenses than girls. Like, Justin needs money to pay for his girlfriend when they go out on dates. Oh yeah, and he's saving up to buy a car." Carmen paused. "Never mind that I have to save up my salary to help pay for college!"

"That doesn't sound very fair," Jung said. "I mean, isn't it illegal to pay someone more money just because of their sex?"

"If it isn't, it should be," Amanda added.

"I think you should quit," Jung suggested. "If you don't like the way they are treating you, then stop working there."

"I wish I could quit," Carmen sighed. "But I need this job. And it makes me mad that all the other girls would still be getting unfair treatment. I don't know what to do."

Sex Discrimination at Work

Carmen's problem is very common. On average, women make 75 cents for every $1.00 men make *for the same work.* The current workplace environment has been shaped by years of stereotyped thinking about the sexes. Just as society tends to value men and traditionally masculine traits over women and traditionally feminine traits, society tends to value men's work over women's. This is expressed in financial terms, that is, lower salaries for women.

Another reason that men generally earn more than women for the same work is that men have been socialized to be assertive and women passive. Men often demand—and thus receive—more money from their employers.

In addition, when hiring women or assessing whether to give women raises, many employers burden female workers with assumptions that they do not impose on their male employees. For instance, some employers may believe that women who work are just passing time until they "settle down" and have children. When a working couple does have children, these employers wonder if a working mother, not a working father, will quit her job or cut back on her hours so that she can take care of the children. They fear that they will "waste" training on a female employee who is likely to leave. Other employers may assume that women work as a hobby rather than to support their families and thus do not deserve to be paid as much as "serious" employees.

But the truth is, more women must work to support themselves and their families. The two-income family is the norm. In this economic climate, in which roughly 50 percent of the workforce is women, it is relatively unlikely that a woman will leave her job to raise her family.

The "wage gap" between men and women exists even in traditionally "female" professions, such as nursing, social work, and elementary school teaching. Men in these fields tend to rise more quickly, make more money, and hold higher positions than their female coworkers.

In addition to being paid less for the same work, women have been segregated into lower paying jobs. In 1990, women made up 45.5 percent of the workforce, but most were stuck in low-paying jobs such as clerical workers, nurse's aides, food service workers, and retail salespeople. These jobs, sometimes called "pink-collar work," are the female equivalent of "blue-collar" work, which is done primarily by men. For the most part, pink-collar jobs are lower in status and lower paying than blue-collar jobs. In fact, one of the main differences between pink- and blue-collar jobs is that pink-collar jobs require more education and skill. Ironically, blue-collar jobs pay more money.

The good news is that the situation is slowly starting to change. The number of women entering traditionally male-dominated fields is increasing. Today, approximately 40 percent of all law degrees and 33 percent of all medical and MBA degrees are earned by women. Women in business make up 40 percent of all executive, management, and administrative positions. Still, on average, women in these fields make less money and hold lower-status positions than their male coworkers.

"Women's Work"

"I thought women were finally supposed to have equal rights in the workplace," Amanda told Carmen and Jung. "It seems like nothing has changed."

"Come on, Amanda," Jung exclaimed. "Things are changing. After all, my mother is a lawyer, and your mom owns her own auto repair business."

"Yeah, I'm proud of my mom," Amanda agreed, "but it hasn't been easy. One of the reasons she decided to start her own business was because she was sick of having to put up with bosses who were sexist. When she was starting out, lots of people refused to hire her as a mechanic because she was a woman."

"Wow," Carmen exclaimed.

"My mother complains about it too," Jung said. "She says that a lot of law firms still don't take women lawyers seriously. They think that women

71

are not aggressive enough to handle the really big cases, or that all women want to do family law."

"Yeah," Amanda joined in, "and when women do act aggressive or ambitious they are put down for being too masculine!"

"A lot of people believe that work outside the home is not as important to women as it is to men," Jung said. "When my mother was pregnant with my younger sister, everyone at her firm thought that she would quit once the baby was born. They were really surprised when she came back to work, even though she had told them she would be back."

"You know, I thought things were basically equal," Carmen said. "I never thought that I'd have to deal with sex discrimination at work."

Gender stereotypes can lead to different expectations for male and female employees. Research shows that in the male-dominated field of business, women tend to be viewed more negatively than their male coworkers. Supervisors are more likely to back up a man's decision than a woman's. Some men also have trouble relating to women in the workplace. They are used to thinking of women as girlfriends, wives, or lovers, but not as peers. Personality traits such as aggressiveness, which are valued in men in professions like business and law, are not always considered "suitable" traits for women. This can create a difficult situation for women in these fields, who may be criticized for not being aggressive enough or may alternately be considered "too" aggressive. In other fields, too, employers may impose different standards on male and female employees.

Lookism

When Carmen came home from work she found her older sister, Yvonne, sitting at the kitchen table picking at a piece of cake.

"I could use a hunk of that," Carmen said.

"Rough day?" Yvonne asked.

"You've got that right!" Carmen exclaimed with a sigh. Then she told her sister about Justin. Yvonne didn't seem surprised.

"It's just another case of sex discrimination," Yvonne said in an ironic tone. "I know how you feel. Something similar happened to me once." Carmen wondered why her sister had never mentioned it.

"Remember that diner where I used to work?" Yvonne continued.

Carmen nodded. "I remember. You quit because the manager was a jerk."

"He was a jerk, all right," Yvonne said. "He was always bugging me about the way I looked. You know, like he'd tell me that I should wear more make-up and fix up my hair so I would be more attractive to the male customers. The last straw was when he bought these skimpy uniforms for the waitresses. I overheard him saying that they would bring in more customers. When I complained that my uniform didn't fit me, he told me that was because I was too fat and that if I wanted to keep working there I should lose some weight. I felt terrible!"

"Ugh. I understand why you decided to quit," Carmen said. "But how is that sex discrimination?"

"Well, my manager never bugged any of the waiters

73

about their appearance," Yvonne explained. "It was like he had different standards for the male and female employees. The waitresses had to look sexy, but the waiters just had to do their jobs."

"I see what you mean," Carmen said with a nod. "He didn't expect his male employees to wear skimpy outfits so that they would attract women customers."

"Exactly. And that's why it's sex discrimination," Yvonne said. "I only wish I had realized that at the time. Then maybe I would have stood up to the manager rather than quitting my job."

Yvonne's story illustrates a more subtle form of sex discrimination. Lookism is discrimination against a person on the basis of his or her physical appearance. Our society places a great deal of importance on appearances. The media are full of images of fit, attractive people selling products, acting in movies, and even delivering the nightly news.

In our society, a man's worth is generally judged by his abilities and accomplishments. A woman's worth is often judged by her physical appearance in a way that a man's is not.

This message is conveyed loud and clear by the media. In magazines, on television, and in the movies, the majority of women are young, fit, and attractive. The men, on the other hand, come in a variety of shapes and sizes, some of them older or overweight. Think about it: Have you ever seen a woman who is not young, thin, and attractive anchoring the news? Probably not. In fact, female anchors are sometimes fired or demoted because of their age or their weight. A completely different standard exists for men. Not only are older and overweight men on the news, but as a male news anchor ages he is seen as having more authority and experience.

Lookism can occur in any profession. Many people believe that attractive women are more intelligent and competent than unattractive women, or that overweight women must be lazy and unambitious. Ironically, in some cases, being attractive can also be a disadvantage in the workplace. Some men have trouble taking attractive women seriously. They think of women as sex objects, not coworkers.

These biased ideas can affect how women are treated on the job. They can even affect whether or not a woman is hired in the first place. Lookism in hiring or work performance is sex discrimination when males and females are subjected to different standards of appearance with respect to their work.

Unfortunately, many people don't take lookism very seriously. Sexist ideas about appearance are so deeply entrenched in our society that many people still think it's okay to discriminate against women on the basis of physical appearance.

Know Your Rights

To prevent sex discrimination in the workplace, it is important for people to understand the law. Two main federal laws forbid sex discrimination in employment: The Equal Pay Act (EPA) of 1963 and Title VII of the Civil Rights Act of 1964. Both the EPA and Title VII are enforced by the federal EEOC and each state's Fair Employment Practices Agency (FEPA).

The EPA makes it illegal for employers to pay different wages to male and female employees who "perform substantially equal work under similar working conditions in the same establishment."

Title VII prohibits employment discrimination of any kind based on sex, race, color, religion, or national origin. Together these laws give men and women the right to equal pay for equal work.

Same Job, Different Salary

Jung couldn't believe that anyone could get away with paying males and females different salaries for the same work. When Jung's mother came home from work, he told her about Carmen's problem and asked what Carmen should do.

Minny Cho, who was an attorney, listened. "Carmen's problem is very common," she said.

"So it is illegal to pay males and females different salaries for the same job?" Jung asked.

"Absolutely."

"So, how does Carmen's boss get away with it?" Jung asked.

"Well, for one thing, you have to be able to prove that sex discrimination really occurred. Cases like Carmen's are actually the most straightforward. Since Carmen and Justin were hired to do the same job, Carmen just has to be able to show that she and Justin do essentially the same work, but that he gets more money just because he is a boy."

"That sounds easy enough," Jung said.

76

"Then her case should be easy to prove. But it can get a lot more complicated. For instance, the owner could claim that Justin makes more money than the girls because he has more responsibilities. Sometimes employers give different job titles to their male and female employees. Let me give you an example. In a large law firm like mine, we need a lot of people to do filing and typing, and to answer the phones."

"You mean secretaries," Jung broke in.

"Well, it used to be that most of the women who did those jobs were called 'secretaries,' but the men who were hired to do essentially the same job were called 'clerks.'"

"What's the difference?" Jung asked.

"The difference is that the male 'clerks' at my company made more money than the female 'secretaries'," his mother said.

"That can't be the only difference," Jung said.

"The company claimed that the clerks and secretaries had different duties. The secretaries spent more time answering phones, while the clerks had 'more important' responsibilities, like supervising the secretaries."

"So that's why they got more money," Jung said.

"That's not what the court decided," Jung's mother said.

"They went to court?" Jung asked.

"Yes. One of the secretaries sued the company for sex discrimination," Jung's mother explained. "You see, the law doesn't require that two jobs be identical, but 'substantially equal.' In other words, since most of their work was the same, the court decided

that people with the job titles secretary and clerk should be paid the same amount."

"I'm surprised that your company got away with that kind of discrimination in the first place."

More About Title VII

Title VII also protects against discrimination in hiring, firing, work assignments, promotions, layoffs, and use of company facilities. The law requires that equally qualified women and men have equal chances to be hired for a job and to receive raises and promotions.

It is not legal to hire a man over an equally qualified woman just because he is a man. The law requires that job duties be assigned based on ability or seniority, not sex. It is not legal to have female salespeople straightening up the displays while the male salespeople handle the money. According to the law, if both were hired to do the same job, then they should do the same work.

The law requires that from the very first job interview an employer should act as if he or she is wearing a blindfold. The sex of the applicant should be considered irrelevant. That way, the interview as well as all subsequent treatment will be based on qualifications and performance, not on sex.

Title VII identifies two categories of employment discrimination: disparate treatment and disparate impact.

Disparate Treatment
Disparate treatment involves cases in which an employer intentionally treats male and female employees differently.

This includes intentionally paying male and female employees different salaries for the same work or passing over a highly qualified woman and instead promoting a less qualified man.

Carmen's case falls into the disparate treatment category. Her boss knowingly paid her less money than he paid a male coworker doing the same work. He even admitted that he was paying Justin more money than Carmen for no reason than because he was a boy.

Subtler Discrimination: Disparate Impact

"You know, Jung, there's another, more subtle kind of discrimination that is even more difficult to spot," Jung's mother continued. *"In legal language it's called disparate impact. A few years ago, I represented a group of women who sued the fire department for sex discrimination."*

Jung's eyes lit up. *"I remember that case!"* he exclaimed.

"Well," his mother continued, *"before that case, there had never been any female firefighters in the Westbrook Fire Department. No woman had ever been able to pass the test. A lot of women had come close, but none of them was able to pass the strength portion of the test."*

"That doesn't sound like discrimination," Jung said. *"It just sounds like making sure you have good firefighters. If women aren't strong enough to be firefighters, then they shouldn't be."*

"Well, that's the thing. As it turned out, the women were strong enough to be firefighters, even though they couldn't pass the test."

"How do you mean?" Jung asked.

"We were able to show that the abilities measured by the strength test were not the ones necessary to be a good firefighter. An improved strength test could assess the abilities of any candidate, male or female, more accurately. The court ruled that the old test was unfair because its impact or effect was to exclude women from becoming firefighters."

"That's complicated," Jung said.

"It's not really that complicated, once you understand the law," Ms. Cho said. "That's another reason why some employers still get away with sex discrimination—most people just don't know enough about the law."

Defining Disparate Impact

The second type of discrimination that Title VII prohibits is called *disparate impact*. This refers to situations in which the employer intentionally or unintentionally uses certain employment practices that have the effect, or *impact,* of discriminating against employees on the basis of sex. The Westbrook Fire Department was guilty of discrimination because it required employees to pass a strength test that women could not pass even if they were strong enough to be firefighters. In other words, the *impact* of the test was to discriminate against candidates on the basis of sex. In cases of disparate impact discrimination, it does not matter if the employer did not mean to discriminate. It is still discrimination.

Affirmative Action

Title VII also requires that employers who have discriminated against women in the past must make it a goal to end such discrimination. This is part of what is known as *affirmative action.* The purpose of affirmative action is to make up for past discrimination in education and employment opportunities. Recently, affirmative action has been the topic of heated debate.

The Controversy over Affirmative Action

Affirmative action is not a new idea. It has been around for more than thirty years. You have probably heard of affirmative action. But, like many people, you may be confused about what it is.

Affirmative action is the name given to a wide variety of means for increasing employment and educational opportunities for women and minorities. This includes, for instance, special programs to recruit women and training programs to help women and minorities develop skills necessary for school or employment. Affirmative action can also apply to decisions about whom to hire for a job, or whom to admit to a selective university. For example, if it can be shown that a company hired qualified men over equally qualified women just because they were men, that company may be required to set a goal of hiring more women in the future.

Affirmative Action Is Introduced

The concept of affirmative action was first developed by President Lyndon B. Johnson. President Johnson was aware of the "old boys' network." The network was a group of powerful men who knew each other socially and professionally. Many were employers. Employers needing new staff would often hire relatives of their friends or friends of their friends, rather than fairly considering all candidates or even making it possible for women and minorities to apply. As a result, most of the people hired through this network were white males. Johnson was also aware of the racism within American society that prevented many people from being hired because they were not white.

In 1965, President Johnson issued Executive Order 11246, which prohibited federal agencies from doing business with firms that were not committed to equal opportunity for people of all races, colors, religions, and national origins. In his eyes, the commitment to equal opportunity meant that companies should not only end discrimination, but that they should make an active effort to give minorities the jobs and educational opportunities from which they had been intentionally or unintentionally excluded in the past. In a famous speech at Howard University in 1965, President Johnson said:

"Freedom is not enough. You do not wipe away the scars of centuries. You do not take a man who for years has been hobbled by chains, liberate him, and bring him to the starting line of a race saying 'you are free to compete with all others,' and still justly believe you have been completely fair. Thus it is not enough to open the gates of opportunity."

At first the concept of affirmative action was specifically targeted to benefit African Americans, whose civil rights had only recently been secured under Title VII in 1964. The idea was later extended to other minorities. In 1967 President Johnson issued another Executive Order, EO 11375, which extended affirmative action to women.

As the president had envisioned, affirmative action opened up many new opportunities for women and minorities in the workplace. Between 1970 and 1990 the proportion of women doctors jumped from 7.6 percent to 16.9 percent. There were similar increases in the numbers of women becoming lawyers, accountants, judges, and school administrators. Between 1987 and 1997, the number of black professional women grew 125 percent. In California between 1975 and 1993 the percentage of African-Americans and Latinos who held high-level positions in major companies rose from 4.8 percent to 8.3 percent.

Criticism of Affirmative Action

Since the time President Johnson's orders were put into effect, much has changed. Progress has been made, with women and minorities enjoying more opportunities than in the past. Much remains to be done, however, in establishing fair and equal treatment.

At the same time, the political climate of the United States has changed. Many people feel that enough compensation has been made for past discrimination and that it is time to remove the advantage that affirmative action has given women and minorities. Many now consider what was originally intended as compensation for unfair past biases to be itself unfair bias in the present. Opponents of affirmative action assert that it is "reverse discrimination." They claim that affirmative action discriminates against white men. This is an understandable accusation. Significantly, however, only 2 percent of the 91,000 employment discrimination cases ever filed with the EEOC concern reverse discrimination. Even with affirmative action in place, the vast majority of cases still involve discrimination against women and minorities.

Another common criticism of affirmative action is that it involves using "quotas." Many people believe that under affirmative action companies must hire a certain number of women or minorities even if the people they hire are not qualified for the job.

In fact, affirmative action programs cannot use quotas, because the use of quotas is against the law. In the 1978 case of *Bakke v. University of California*, the U.S. Supreme Court ruled that the University of California Medical School could no longer reserve 16 of its 100 places for minority students. The court decided that it was unconstitutional to base an admissions decision solely on the race of the applicant. On the other hand, the court found that it was acceptable to consider race as long as it was not the only factor. The court also ruled that such "race-conscious" selection processes are allowed only in cases where it can be shown that the school has been guilty of discrimination in the past.

The issue of "race-conscious" selection is by far the most controversial aspect of affirmative action. Many people believe that in a truly fair system, employers and universities should not pay any attention at all to race or sex.

Some opponents of affirmative action believe that it was once useful but should now be abandoned. Others believe that affirmative action actually undermines women and minorities: A woman or member of a minority group can never be sure if he or she was hired because of being qualified or because of affirmative action. Coworkers or fellow students may also view such a person as having been hired or accepted on the basis of lower standards.

Challenging Affirmative Action

During the past few years the controversy over affirmative action has intensified. In November 1996, a majority of California citizens voted yes on Proposition 209. The purpose of Proposition 209 is to end all forms of affirmative action in California. The law prohibits affirmative action programs in public employment, education, and contracting. The initiative even legalizes some forms of sex discrimination: One clause of the initiative states that it is legal to exclude women from certain jobs and contracts if it is "reasonably necessary." Proposition 209 was approved by 54 percent of California voters. Those in favor of affirmative action, including President Bill Clinton, were shocked. They worried that other states would follow California's example and ban affirmative action programs.

Advocates of affirmative action may have reason to be concerned. The House Judiciary Committee has been working on a federal version of Proposition 209. This legislation would prohibit the federal government from granting preferences to women and minorities in hiring, contracting, and other programs. And recently, several states—including Washington, Texas, and Michigan—have started campaigns to end affirmative action. Others seek to maintain it. In November 1997, voters in Houston, Texas, approved a measure in favor of continuing the city's affirmative action programs. But affirmative action won by a narrow margin: Fifty-five percent voted to continue it, and 45 percent voted to end it.

What is the future of affirmative action? No one knows for sure. Immediately following the 1996 election supporting

Proposition 209 in California, the American Civil Liberties Union (ACLU) filed a lawsuit against the state of California. It argued that Proposition 209 violated the Fourteenth Amendment of the United States Constitution, which prohibits discrimination based on race and sex in employment, contracting, and education. Chief U.S. District Court Judge Thelton E. Henderson agreed with the ACLU's argument that Proposition 209 was unconstitutional.

But the state of California appealed this decision, and the judges for the Ninth Circuit Court of Appeals ruled that Proposition 209 was constitutional. The U.S. Supreme Court has decided not to hear an appeal of the case. For now at least, Proposition 209 is being implemented in California.

It is hard to predict what will happen next. If other states follow California's lead, it could mean the end of affirmative action. Chances are, however, that the final decision will eventually be made by the Supreme Court.

Sex discrimination in the workplace is a complex problem. Even with programs like affirmative action, the problem has lessened, but it has not gone away.

Sexual Harassment

As soon as the coach blew the whistle, the players raced off the soccer field toward the locker rooms. Samantha, who played halfback, led the group. She was an excellent sprinter. In fact, with her speed and aggressiveness on the field she was sure to be voted most valuable player. As she raced past the fence near the parking lot, a group of boys started yelling and whistling at her.

"Nice legs," one of the boys shouted.

"Hey, Sam, nice buns," another boy joined in.

Samantha picked up her pace. They had been hassling her all through practice. She had tried to ignore it, but they wouldn't quit.

"Leave me alone," she shouted back at them. But they started laughing as if it were a joke. Samantha had a sick feeling in the pit of her stomach.

Samantha's friend Angel was waiting for her near the entrance to the gym. Angel was new to the school, but in the few months he had been there he and Samantha had become good friends. Samantha nearly ran past him.

"Hey, Sam!" Angel called out. "Take it easy. Practice is over!"

Samantha turned and saw Angel. Her expression was tense.

"Are you okay?" he asked.

"Did you hear those guys?" Samantha asked. "They've been hassling me all week. It's hard to concentrate on my game."

Angel had noticed the boys shouting at Samantha and some of the other girls. But he didn't take it too seriously. "You shouldn't let guys like that bother you," he said. "If anything, you should take it as a compliment. They think you're cute."

Samantha looked Angel squarely in the face. "Sexual harassment isn't a compliment," she said.

"Sexual harassment?" Angel look surprised and a little dubious. "I thought sexual harassment was when a male boss made a female employee sleep with him in order to get a promotion."

"It's any kind of unwanted and unreturned sexual attention. It doesn't have to be from your boss or teacher to be harassment."

"C'mon, Sam, you really mean to tell me that a few guys telling you that you're cute means that they are harassing you?"

"Yes, because they don't respect me enough to leave me alone when I ask them to. It makes me hate going out onto the field, knowing they're going to hassle me," Samantha replied. "I'm going to complain to the coach."

Angel listened but shrugged his shoulders. It seemed like a lot of noise over something that wasn't such a big deal.

Was It Sexual Harassment?

Was Samantha the victim of sexual harassment? Yes. Sexual harassment is defined as deliberate sexual behavior that is neither asked for nor returned. In this case, Samantha did not ask for the boys' attention, and she did not return it. Calling out unwanted comments about someone's appearance is an example of sexual harassment. Here are some other behaviors that may be considered harassment if they are unwanted and unreturned:

- Sexual teasing, jokes, remarks, or gestures

- Pressure for dates

- Letters, phone calls, or material of a sexual nature

- Being made the subject of sexual rumors

- Having one's clothes pulled in a sexual way

- Being shown or given unwanted pictures or notes

- Sexually suggestive looks or gestures

- Mooning or flashing

- Deliberate touching, brushing up against, leaning over, cornering, or pinching

- Pressure for sexual favors

- Being forced to kiss someone

- Being called gay or lesbian

89

↪ Being spied on while showering or dressing at school

↪ Attempted rape or sexual assault

You may be surprised to learn that some of the above behaviors are sexual harassment. Perhaps you have been the victim of sexual harassment without even realizing it. Maybe you were walking home from school when a group of men made catcalls or whistled at you. Or maybe an uncle said something about your physical appearance that made you uncomfortable.

Sometimes it can be hard to distinguish between sexual harassment and friendly flirting, but there are differences. Unlike flirting, sexual harassment is not about sexuality, it is about power. Harassment is usually intended to intimidate. It is not a compliment. In addition, when people flirt the sexual attention is usually mutual. But with sexual harassment the attention is one-sided.

Samantha did not feel flattered by the boys' sexual comments, and she did not return the attention. In fact, Samantha made it clear that the boys' behavior was upsetting her, and she even asked them to stop. If her harassers had meant only to be friendly, they would have stopped when they realized that their comments were unwelcome.

You can usually tell the difference between flirting and harassment. First, flirting generally makes you feel good, whereas sexual harassment makes you feel uncomfortable. For example, when someone you like tells you that you look attractive in the outfit you are wearing you feel good. But when your teacher tells you that you look "sexy in those pants" you may feel uncomfortable or embarrassed. From a teacher, that kind of attention is inappropriate.

Second, flirting is always a compliment, and it should never feel like a putdown. For example, if a stranger tells you that you have "a great set of breasts," the words may sound like a compliment but feel more like a putdown. You didn't ask for the stranger's opinion, and chances are you were not interested in hearing his judgment of your body.

Finally, flirting should never make you feel frightened. If you feel that one of your superiors is threatening you ("You know, people who don't show enough loyalty to their superiors don't usually get promoted") or making you feel uncomfortable, you may be a victim of sexual harassment.

Sexual harassment can happen anywhere—at work, in school, or on the street. Often the harasser is someone in authority, such as a teacher, a boss, or a religious leader, but he or she may also be a peer, or even a stranger. Harassment victims, like the harassers themselves, come in all ages, races, and socioeconomic backgrounds. The majority of harassment victims are women, but no one is immune to sexual harassment.

Harassment in the Workplace

Thanks to Anita Hill, the problem of sexual harassment in the workplace has received a lot of attention. Sexual harassment occurs in all areas of government, business, academia, and industry. Harassment is common in traditionally female-dominated fields, like nursing and secretarial work. But it is also a problem in male-dominated fields like medicine, government, and law. For instance, in 1992 the American Medical Women's Association surveyed 200 doctors from its Massachusetts chapter. At least one in four female doctors reported that they had been sexually harassed on the job. One-half of the doctors and surgeons reported that they had received unwanted sexual attention and harassment. A 1993 *Washington Post* survey of women working on Capitol Hill found that one third of the respondents had been harassed by coworkers, lobbyists, senators, and congressmen. In the same year, a study conducted by the Seattle City Council's public safety committee found that 80 percent of female police officers had experienced sexual harassment. Sexual harassment affects women at all levels. A 1993 survey of 400 top female executives conducted by the UCLA Graduate School of Management found that two-thirds of the respondents had been sexually harassed.

Sexual harassment makes it even more difficult for women to break into traditionally male-dominated professions. Victims of harassment are often forced to transfer or quit and are sometimes even fired. In the short term, victims may find themselves unemployed or in a lower-paying job. In the long term, leaving a job can mean giving up seniority already built up toward a raise or promotion, as well as health-care benefits. Since the majority of harassment victims are women, sexual harassment contributes to the problem of poverty among women. In addition, women whose coworkers are harassed can suffer from the same low morale, lack of trust, and decreased loyalty to their companies as the victims themselves.

Sexual harassment has significant economic effects on the business community as a whole. It has been estimated that a typical Fortune 500 company loses $6.7 million a year because of sexual harassment. This figure includes losses caused by victims' absence from work and lower productivity, as well as the costs of rehiring and retraining when talented people leave because of harassment. The figure does not include lawsuits filed against companies who failed to protect their employees, which also cost millions.

Harassment at School

"I've been thinking about what you said yesterday," Angel told Samantha the next day at lunch. *"And you know, I think sexual harassment happens all the time at school."*

"Hey, can we join you?" Jon said, sitting down next to them. "What's going on?" Mimi sat down too.

"Angel was saying that he thinks sexual harassment happens a lot here at school," Samantha said.

"Yeah," Angel added, "but people think it's normal behavior."

"What do you mean by sexual harassment?" Mimi asked. "I've never been harassed at school."

"Maybe you have and you just didn't know it," Samantha said. "Like when guys rub against you in the hallways. The guys act like it's funny, but I think it's embarrassing. Or remember that time when those guys starting asking us crude questions about our sex lives?"

Mimi nodded and wrinkled her nose. "That made me really uncomfortable."

"That was sexual harassment," Samantha said.

"You know what really bugs me," Mimi said after a moment, "is when guys 'rate' the girls as we walk into a classroom. It happens a lot in homeroom. It's bad enough that they think of us as sex objects that they can rate—but to do it in front of everyone!"

"That's so rude," Samantha agreed. "Why do guys do that?" she asked Jon and Angel.

"Girls aren't always so innocent," Jon retorted. "I remember once when a certain group of girls spied on Doug and me when we were changing in the locker room." Samantha and Mimi blushed.

"It was just a prank," Mimi said. "We didn't mean anything by it."

Jon continued, "You guys were all 'Hey, let me see!' but you know, that was really embarrassing."

Angel, who had been listening quietly, spoke up.

"Last year I was really upset because a group of guys and girls at my old school started a rumor around school that I was gay. It wasn't true, but a lot of people believed it and started treating me differently." Angel looked down at the floor. "I was so upset that I skipped school for the rest of the week. That's one of the reasons why my family moved."

"Oh, Angel," Samantha said, "that's so unfair."

The Cost of Harassment

As Samantha and her friends discovered, sexual harassment is a serious problem in school. A 1992 survey conducted by the AAUW found that 81 percent of eighth-through eleventh-grade students had experienced some

94

form of sexual harassment. That's four out of every five students. In the majority of these incidents, the harassers were other students. But 25 percent of the girls and 10 percent of the boys reported that they had been harassed by a school employee, such as a teacher, coach, bus driver, or security guard. The most common forms of sexual harassment were unwanted sexual comments, looks, and gestures, as well as sexual touching, grabbing, and pinching. But the students surveyed reported a wide variety of experiences, ranging from sexual rumor to sexual assault.

Recently, the problem of sexual harassment in school has received a lot of attention in the media. In October 1996, the California state court ordered a school district to pay $500,000 in damages to the family of Tianna Ugarte. Her family filed suit after a boy in her class repeatedly called her a "slut" and a "bitch" and threatened her physically. Tianna said that the harassment occurred every day for most of the school year.

In that same year, the family of Eve Bruneau sued New York State's South Kortright school district after a member of her sixth-grade class tormented her so much that she had to move to another school. The Bruneaus complained that a group of boys called Eve and other girls in her class names like "ugly dog-faced bitch" and "whore."

Sexual harassment cases are not limited to harassment of girls by boys. In 1996, a boy filed suit against the California Laguna Salada Union School District after being called "gay" and "faggot" and being physically attacked by students in his class. The boy was so upset by this experience that he lost thirty pounds, began having serious headaches, and even contemplated suicide.

95

In many of these kinds of cases victims claim that their schools did not take their complaints seriously. When Eve Bruneau's mother complained about her daughter's harassment to school officials, they told her that the boys were just flirting.

The problem is that the majority of students, teachers, and administrators do not understand how serious the problem of sexual harassment really is. The AAUW found that many students believe that sexual harassment is "a normal part of school life," and that "it's no big deal." Many adults believe that harassment is just a normal, harmless part of adolescent flirting.

Despite such beliefs, sexual harassment is neither "normal" nor "harmless." The AAUW report found that nearly one in four victims skipped school or cut a class after experiencing harassment. Victims also reported that they did not want to participate as much in class, had trouble paying attention, and found it hard to study. A small percentage of students even thought about changing schools as a result of sexual harassment.

Sexual harassment affects everyone, not just its victims. When schools permit sexual harassment, they send the message to students that girls are not worthy of respect, and that it is acceptable for boys to put down girls.

Your Legal Rights

Just as many people are confused about how to define sexual harassment, many people are unsure about the laws that protect against it. Legally, sexual harassment is a form of sex discrimination. Sexual harassment is unlawful because harassers treat individuals differently based on their sex. The same laws that protect against other forms of sex discrimination protect against sexual harassment.

Your Rights at School

Title IX of the Education Act of 1972 prohibits sexual harassment in school. The Office of Civil Rights (OCR) of the U.S. Department of Education is responsible for enforcing Title IX. The OCR recognizes both adult-student and student-student harassment as violations of Title IX. If a school is found guilty of allowing sexual harassment, it can lose its federal funding.

In an effort to curb sexual harassment in schools, the OCR requires that schools develop special policies for dealing with harassment. Schools are required to develop grievance procedures for handling sexual harassment complaints. They are also required to designate an employee to be responsible for the school's Title IX responsibilities. Information about the school's sexual harassment policies and procedures must be made public, and students should know who the school's Title IX officer is.

Unfortunately, schools have been slow to comply with this regulation. According to a study by the National Organization of Women (NOW) and Wellesley College, only 8 percent of the schools surveyed have policies for dealing with sexual harassment. The study also found that schools without established policies are less likely to take action against harassment complaints.

The OCR prohibits sexual harassment of a student by a school employee such as a teacher. In fact, in most cases, the OCR considers any sexual contact between a student and an adult employee to be sexual harassment, even if the contact is consensual.

The court system, too, holds schools responsible for adult-student harassment. In 1992, the U.S. Supreme Court ruled that school districts could be sued for damages for violating Title IX. The landmark case, *Franklin v. Gwinnett Public Schools*, arose when a high school student complained that a sexually aggressive teacher had harassed and seduced her. School officials had been warned several times about the teacher's pursuit of female students, but they did nothing. The court ruled that the school district was liable for the harassment.

Over the past few years there has been some controversy about whether schools can be held responsible for student-to-student harassment. Some schools have argued that they cannot control what students do among themselves, or that it is too difficult to distinguish between normal adolescent behavior and sexual harassment.

But in 1997, the OCR released a new set of Title IX guidelines concerning student-to-student harassment. According to the OCR, unwelcome sexual advances, requests for sexual favors, and other verbal and physical conduct of a sexual nature constitute sexual harassment when the conduct is severe, persistent, and pervasive enough to limit a student's ability to participate in or benefit from the education program or to create a hostile or abusive environment. The OCR will hold schools responsible for creating a hostile environment if they know the problem exists and fail to take appropriate action to remedy the situation.

Although the OCR treats both adult-to-student and student-to-student forms of harassment as violations of Title IX, the court system has interpreted the laws differently. Some state courts have awarded monetary damages to victims of student-to-student harassment, but not all courts agree.

In 1996, the U.S. Court of Appeals for the Fifth Circuit ruled that school districts cannot be held liable for failing to control sexual harassment by peers. In the same year, the U.S. Court of Appeals for the Eleventh Circuit made a similar decision.

Most experts agree that this issue will eventually be resolved by the U.S. Supreme Court. So far, however, it has refused to hear any appeals for cases of student-to-student harassment.

Your Rights at Work

In the workplace, Title VII of the Civil Rights Act of 1964 makes it illegal to discriminate against employees on the basis of sex. This law gives all employees the right to work in an environment that is free of intimidation, insult, or ridicule based on sex. The law requires employers to pro-tect their employees from being harassed. Employers can be held responsible for sexual harassment if they know-ingly allow it, or if they could have prevented it from occurring. Title VII gives victims the right to sue individu-als who harass them, as well as their companies for not protecting them from the harassment.

Title VII is enforced by the Equal Employment Opportunity Commission (EEOC). The EEOC recognizes two main categories of sexual harassment: *quid pro quo*, and creating a *hostile environment*.

Quid pro quo is a Latin term that means "something given in return for something else." It applies to cases in which a superior, such as a boss or a teacher, demands sexual favors from a subordinate as a condition for keeping a job or receiving a raise, promotion, or good grade. These are the most clear-cut cases to argue in court. Courts often hold the employer responsible even if he or she was not aware that sexual harassment had taken place, although such decisions are increasingly being challenged.

The term sexual harassment used to be reserved for *quid pro quo* cases. But in recent years the interpretation of the law has been extended to protect employees from any form of unwelcome sexual conduct that creates a *hostile* work environment.

A hostile environment is one in which an employee feels neither comfortable nor welcome because of his or her sex. Repeated sexual behaviors such as telling sexually explicit jokes, making vulgar, abusive, suggestive, or overtly sexual comments can make employees uncomfortable and can therefore create a hostile environment. The sexual behavior may be merely insensitive or it may be intended to intimidate. Either way, employers can be held responsible for sexual harassment if they knew about the harassment and did nothing to stop it. Even if they did not know, they may also be considered liable if they should have known.

Has It Gone Too Far?

Some people believe that the fight against sexual harassment has gone too far. Critics argue that concepts such as hostile environment are ambiguous and that it is impossible to draw the line between normal behavior and sexual harassment. They cite examples such as that of a six-year-old boy who was suspended from school after he kissed a girl in his class on the cheek, and the University of Nebraska graduate student who was forced to remove from his desk a photograph of his wife in a bikini because other students complained that it violated the school's sexual harassment policy.

But those who support sexual harassment law point out that critics of the law, as well as the media, tend to focus on such controversial cases and ignore many clear-cut cases of harassment that the laws were established to prevent.

Some also argue that sexual harassment laws violate an individual's right to free speech; after all, the U.S. Constitution guarantees all citizens the right to express themselves even if others find their speech offensive. Should an employee have the right to tell a dirty joke at work, even if not everyone agrees that it's funny? Proponents of sexual harassment law counter that we need to balance the right of free expression with the right to fair and equal treatment.

Sexual Harassment, Gender Bias, and Men

"You guys will never guess what just happened," Kevin told a group of his guy friends who were hanging out in the hallway near their lockers. He looked really annoyed. "George and some other guys were suspended because somebody said that they sexually harassed the girls' soccer team!"

"What?" Jim asked. "What happened?"

"I'm not sure," Kevin said. "George said they were only flirting. But I guess Principal Turner didn't see it that way."

"I overheard a group of girls talking about that," Eric broke in."I didn't get all of the details, but they were going on and on about how this was harassment and that was harassment. The way they told the story, it was like everywhere you look some guy is harassing some girl."

"That's so ridiculous," Jim agreed. "So, sexual harassment happens every once in a while. Big deal. I'm sick of girls turning these things into bigger deals than they are."

"Yeah," said Eric. "But did you hear about Mr. Moore, the chemistry teacher? He was fired because he came on to one of the girls in his class."

"Fine, but I'm sick of taking the rap for what other guys do!" Kevin said. "It's like those girls were blaming all guys for just a few bad seeds."

"Exactly!" Eric agreed. "It's not fair. Most guys don't harass girls."

Sexual Harassment and Men

Eric was right when he suggested that most men do not harass women. Although it is true that most sexual harassers are men, it is not true that most men are harassers. Most men respect women and try to avoid harassment. And of those men who do harass women, only a small proportion do it intentionally. Most harassment occurs because people are insensitive or uninformed. In fact, many experts believe that the majority of cases of sexual harassment could be prevented if people were better educated about the issues.

Why do some men harass women? First, it is important to realize that until very recently, sexual harassment and discrimination were legal. In fact, some forms were even considered to be normal. Until the 1960s there were laws to prevent employers from paying men and women the same salaries. The idea was that it was unfair to pay men and women equal wages because men had to support their families. Other laws that were intended to "protect" women from dangerous or "unfit" work actually had the effect of keeping women out of higher-paying jobs.

Sexual harassment results from the way men in our society are socialized. Traditionally, young men and boys are taught that they are supposed to initiate sexual behavior. They learn cultural myths: that women always play "hard to get," and that "when a women says no she really means yes." Women as well as men can reinforce these ideas. A mother who excuses her son's poor treatment of girls or women by simply saying "Boys will be boys!" is telling him that such behavior is acceptable, even expected.

As a result, men sometimes get the message that women want to be aggressively pursued. Occasionally friendly flirting can escalate into sexual harassment because a man does not recognize or ignores the signals that a women is not interested. Many men are used to viewing women as sex objects. They do not think of women as peers, coworkers, or superiors. Many men believe that it's appropriate to sexualize what should be a nonsexual relationship and that, in fact, there is no other choice.

It is difficult for both men and women, as sexual beings, simply to leave sex out of it. However, most men and women try their best not to cross the line into the area of sexual harassment.

Unfortunately, there is a small minority of men who intentionally harass women. These "chronic harassers" do it as a way to assert their power. For men, sex is often associated with power. Experts have found that chronic harassers tend to be older than their victims, married, and of the same race as their victims. They may harass women to boost their own egos or because they enjoy intimidating other people. Some men harass because they feel threatened by women's increasing power in society.

Different Views of Harassment

"Look out, here comes Rita," Eric said in a loud voice. Rita didn't say anything. She kept walking down the hallway toward her locker. Eric was obviously trying to get her attention, and it wasn't working. The other boys seemed amused. Paige, who was standing near-by, did not look amused.

"Yo, Rita, you sure look hot today," Eric continued as he watched Rita work the combination to her lock-er. Rita still didn't answer. She kept her eyes fixed on the dial of the lock. She was flustered by the atten-tion, and she couldn't get the lock open.

"Rita, Rita," Eric sang. "She's so lovely, yet so shy."

When the lock finally snapped open Rita shoved her books into the locker, pulled out the folder for her next class, and took off down the hall without saying a word. She looked upset. Eric was surprised.

"What's her problem?" he mused aloud to his friends. "I was only joking with her. "

"You know girls, they always take everything so seriously," Kevin said.

"Maybe it's 'that time of the month,'" another boy added. Everyone laughed—except Paige.

"I think you're the one with the problem," Paige said to Eric. "It's obvious that Rita isn't interested."

"Oh, she was just acting shy," Eric replied. He looked at his friends for reassurance. One laughed, but none of them said anything.

"You don't know when to quit, do you?" Paige said. "You think you're so smooth, but you're just being rude."

"Hey, wait a minute," Eric protested. "I was just being friendly."

"I saw the whole thing," Paige responded. "Rita tried to ignore you, and you just kept hassling her."

"Now, wait a minute," Kevin said, "I saw the whole thing too. He wasn't hassling her." Eric was glad that someone was finally standing up for him.

"I'll bet Rita thought he was. Why do you think she walked by without even looking at him?" Paige asked. Eric looked doubtful.

"You guys are pathetic," Paige said. "I gotta go to class."

What happened between Eric and Rita explains why sexual harassment sometimes occurs: Males and females have different views of harassment. What may seem like innocent behavior to a man may be considered harassment by a women. Consider the following example.

A male boss invites one of his female employees to lunch to "discuss her work." But while at the restaurant, he does not show any interest in discussing work at all. Instead, he asks her questions about her personal life. The two have lunch again several times; then one night they meet for dinner and drinks. During dinner the boss tries to fondle the employee.

Do you think that this a case of sexual harassment? If so, when do you think the harassment began? In an important study, psychologist Michelle Paludi asked men and women to judge a similar scenario. She found that both the men and the women agreed that the employee had been harassed, but they had different opinions about when the harassment began. The majority of women thought that the harassment began during the very first lunch when the boss wanted to discuss the employee's personal life rather than business. In contrast, most of the men thought that the harassment began when the boss tried to fondle the employee.

In another study, researcher Barbara Gutek examined sex differences in men's and women's reactions to the idea of being propositioned by a coworker. She found that the majority of men, but only a small percentage of women, said that they would be flattered if a coworker propositioned them at work.

Clearly, on average, men and women have different views about the appropriateness of injecting sex into the workplace environment. There could be many reasons behind this, among them the fact that most women want to be taken seriously at work. Unwanted sexual attention in the workplace reinforces the idea that women are sex objects and not persons worthy of respect.

In parallel fashion, the law recognizes that men and women have different views of sexual harassment. Courts have adopted the "reasonable woman" standard for judging sexual harassment cases. When judging whether a certain behavior is harassment, courts ask how a *reasonable woman* would interpret the behavior. Courts also use this standard when judging how seriously a victim was affected by harassment. In this way, the courts take into account that behavior that might be considered harmless by a man may be considered harassment by a woman. Where women's and men's points of view differ, the court uses the woman's point of view for judging the case.

How to Avoid Harassing Women

Sometimes men harass women without even realizing it. They may think that they are just flirting or being friendly. Or they may just be unaware. Many men do not realize when their behavior makes women feel uncomfortable or upset. The most important thing you can do to avoid being the perpetrator of sexual harassment is to learn more about the issues. Reading this book is a good start.

There other are things that you can do. First, if you are unsure about whether or not a certain behavior is harassing, you should assume that it is. It is always better to be safe than sorry. As has already been discussed, men and women can view the same behavior very differently. Do not assume that, just because you meant a comment as a compliment or you thought a dirty joke was funny, the women you know would feel the same way. If you believe that a behavior might offend or upset a woman, it's best not to test your theory.

A second rule for avoiding harassment is always to assume that no means no. Men are often taught that women play "hard to get," but in most cases that is not true. It is always best to assume that a woman means what she says. If she is interested, she will let you know.

Finally, remember that males and females have different views when it comes to sexual harassment. When in doubt, it's always a good idea to seek out the female perspective. Ask your female friends and family members. By discussing the issues you will gain a better understanding of women's viewpoints.

When Men Are Victims

That Friday night, Eric and some of his friends were hanging out at the pizzeria. Eric mentioned what had happened with Rita and wondered aloud if he had been out of line. "I know Paige thought I was," he said.

"You know," Jim said, "I bet it's not just girls who are victims of harassment. I bet there are some guys who have been victims too." The other guys nodded.

"I think I might have been harassed," Jamal said, trying to sound casual. But as soon as he had said it, he wished he could take it back.

No one said anything. Finally Eric asked, "By whom? How come you never said anything?"

"I guess I was embarrassed," Jamal said. "I never even thought of it as harassment. It wasn't really a big deal or anything. "

"So come on," Kevin said. "Let's hear it."

"Well," Jamal started, "it happened last year when I was working at Gerwin's Grocers. There was a woman customer who was always giving me a lot of attention. You know, she would get on the checkout line where I was working and she would ask me to carry her bags for her, and she would give me really big tips."

"Doesn't sound like harassment to me," Kevin broke in. Jamal continued. "She always made comments about how strong and cute I was. It made me feel really uncomfortable. Then one day, she really came on to me in the parking lot. She asked me if I had a girlfriend, and when I said I didn't, she asked me to come to her house and help her unpack her groceries."

"'Unpack her groceries,' hmm!" Kevin said.

"What did you do?" asked Eric.

"Nothing," Jamal said. "I was totally floored. I didn't know what to say. I just turned around and started back toward the store."

"You should have taken her up on it," Kevin said, winking.

"Yeah, like you would have," Jamal said, frowning. "Anyway, I wasn't interested. I don't know why she came on so strong. I mean, I never flirted back."

"So you're telling me that a woman comes on to you, and you're too chicken to do anything about it, but that's sexual harassment?" Jim asked.

"Well, I kept giving her the message that I wasn't interested, but she just kept at it," Jamal explained.

"She must have known she was making you uncomfortable," Eric said.

"And that's not even all of it," Jamal continued. "After that time she propositioned me in the parking lot, she was really cold to me. She even complained to the manager about me. She said that I wasn't polite to her. Can you believe that?"

"Why didn't you just tell your boss what happened?" Eric asked.

"Are you crazy? The whole thing was too weird," Jamal said. "I just wanted to forget about it."

Women Harassing Men

In the 1994 movie *Disclosure*, Demi Moore plays a successful businesswoman who sexually harasses a subordinate employee and former boyfriend, played by Michael

Douglas. Moore's character is hurt because Douglas had once rejected her. She devises an elaborate scheme of revenge in which she sexually harasses him and then accuses him of harassing her.

The National Association of Working Women estimates that 90 percent of the sexual harassment cases involve men harassing women, 9 percent involve same-sex harassment (usually men harassing men), and only 1 percent involve women harassing men. The reason sexual harassment by women receives a lot of attention in the media is because it is so rare.

Since sexual harassment is about power, it is possible that harassment by women will increase as women gain more positions of power. But while men are encouraged to be aggressive when it comes to sex, women are not. So even when women are in positions of authority over men, they are less likely to express this power through sexuality.

Still, even though it is rare, men are sometimes the victims of harassment. In the workplace, a female boss may want to have a sexual relationship with a male subordinate. In school, girls tease boys about their physical appearance, or sexuality, or a female teacher may want a sexual relationship with a student. In 1997, Mary Kay Letourneau, a school teacher in Seattle, pleaded guilty to statutory rape after having a sexual relationship with a thirteen-year-old student and bearing his child.

Same-Sex Harassment

Until recently, sexual harassment lawsuits concerning harassment by people of the same sex have been rejected by courts or have been limited to cases in which a heterosexual employee has complained of harassment by a homosexual coworker. Recently, however, the application of Title VII protection against sexual harassment in the workplace has been expanded.

Joseph Oncale, an oil rig worker, brought a lawsuit against his former employer and three members of his all-male crew, one of whom was his supervisor. Oncale claimed that he had been singled out for unwanted sex play and unwanted touching and had been threatened with rape. As a result of his case, the U.S. Supreme Court had to determine whether federal law concerning sexual harassment protects employees from being sexually harassed at work by people of the same sex.

In March 1998 the Supreme Court unanimously ruled that Title VII does cover same-sex harassment in the workplace. Their ruling will further influence the application of sexual harassment law.

Impact of Sexual Harassment

Research shows that men and women are affected differently by sexual harassment. Male victims of harassment tend to suffer less than their female counterparts. They are less likely to blame themselves for what happened or to become depressed. Men are also less likely than women to quit a job, seek a transfer, or be fired as a result of sexual harassment.

Men are not immune to other forms of sex discrimination either. As discussed earlier, teachers often expect boys to misbehave, and so boys are more likely to get in trouble for poor behavior. In the same way, men in our society face a great deal of pressure to live up to rigid sex-role stereotypes. As a result, boys and men are not given the opportunity to explore stereotypically "female" activities.

In the workplace, society looks down on men who enter "female" fields. Sometimes men are even excluded from traditionally female jobs such as child care and elementary school teaching because people assume that if a man wants to do this kind of work there must be something wrong with him.

Sexual harassment and gender bias affect both men and women. Discrimination prevents both males and females from reaching their full potential in school. In the workplace, discrimination prevents employees from finding the jobs that best suit them and employers from hiring the people best suited for the job. When a boy's or man's mother, sister, girlfriend, or daughter is a victim, he may suffer along with her. No one is immune to the effects of sexual harassment and discrimination.

What You Can Do

"This is the best party I've been to all year," Marla shouted over the music to Gina. "There are so many cute guys here."

Gina didn't answer. She was busy scanning the crowd looking for Rick Lee. She had had a crush on him since grade school.

"Um, I thought I saw Rick a few minutes ago over near the fireplace talking to Wally," Marla continued. Gina tried to keep her cool, but she couldn't help glancing over in Rick's direction. She caught his eyes, almost by accident, and then flashed him an embarrassed smile. Rick smiled back at her. Gina blushed and looked away.

"Don't look now," Marla whispered, "but I think Rick and Wally are heading over here."

Gina looked out of the corner of her eye. Rick was definitely checking her out, and now he was coming over. She could feel her cheeks getting warm.

"Great party," Rick said as he sat down next to Gina on the couch. Gina couldn't believe this was really happening. She nodded her head and smiled.

Somehow Wally had managed to squeeze in next to Marla on the other side of the couch. He leaned uncomfortably close to her and asked, "So, you girls have plans for afterwards?"

"I'm going home soon," Marla responded in a flat tone, and looked away from him. She tried to move closer to Gina, but there wasn't much room left on the couch.

"But it's still early," Wally said, sliding his hand onto Marla's thigh. "Why do you want to leave so soon?"

Marla didn't answer. She tried to move her leg away from him, but Wally didn't take the hint and left his hand there. Marla was offended. Couldn't he tell that she wasn't interested? She was tempted to say something to him, but she didn't want to make a fuss because Gina and Rick seemed to be hitting it off.

"Uh, I'm outta here," Marla finally said, standing up abruptly. She was relieved to have Wally's hand off of her leg. She spoke to Gina: "I promised my parents that I would be home early tonight."

"What's your problem?" Wally said in a loud voice, getting to his feet. "You think you're too good for me?" Marla could feel people's eyes turn in their direction. She was embarrassed and just wanted to leave.

"You are so stuck up, it makes me sick," Wally said. "Everyone knows that you're the biggest tease in school. You don't fool me, Marla. You don't fool anyone!"

Marla bit her lip and fought back the tears. Rick looked embarrassed. Gina stood up. "Stop harassing my friend!" Gina said in a strong voice. "You have no right to harass Marla or anyone else. No one should have to put up with that!" Gina stared at Wally. "I think you'd better leave now," she said.

Rick stood and said, "C'mon, Wally, let's go." He turned to Gina. "See you Monday."

Wally walked away with Rick. Marla felt relieved—and angry.

Confronting Sexual Harassers

As Gina and Marla discovered, one of the best ways to stop sexual harassment can be to confront a harasser head-on. Confronting the harasser can surprise him and may cause him to back down. It can also help the victim to regain her sense of power and self-esteem. By talking back to the harasser, the victim lets him know that she is unwilling to be victimized. Finally, by confronting the harasser she sends the message that his behavior is not acceptable. He can no longer pretend that he is just flirting or being friendly; he can no longer say that he does not get the message.

Confrontation starts with saying no. It may mean telling your boss that you are not interested in having a sexual relationship, or telling a group of men on the street that you do not appreciate their catcalls.

Unfortunately, confrontation does not come naturally for many women. Most girls are not raised to be assertive or to stand up for themselves. Instead, they are often taught that the best response to unpleasant behavior is to ignore it. Maybe you remember when you were younger, a parent or teacher told you that the boys would stop teasing you if you pretended not to notice them. The problem is that ignoring sexual harassment does not help you. It is painful and hurtful. In most cases ignoring harassment will not make it stop. In

116

fact, by ignoring the behavior you may unintentionally send the message that the harassment is okay.

In her book, *Back Off: How to Confront and Stop Sexual Harassment and Harassers,* Martha Langelan offers some guidelines.

First, Langelan recommends that victims *name the behavior.* State clearly what the harasser has done to offend you, and be specific. For example, tell the harasser, "Stop shouting rude comments about my body," or "Stop asking me for dates when you know I'm not interested." It is important to be honest and direct. Don't exaggerate or downplay the offensive behavior.

Second, it is helpful to *label the behavior as harassment.* For example, tell the harasser, "When you make lewd comments to girls in the hallway, that's sexual harassment." When you label the behavior you let the harasser know that you are not accepting it as flirting or friendly banter.

A third useful strategy for confrontation is to *make it clear that all women should be free from harassment.* Statements such as, "No woman likes to be harassed" lets the harasser know that he is not offending only you, but all women. You make it harder for the harasser to pretend you're the one with the problem, or to accuse you of overreacting.

Finally, *demand that the harassment stop.* Make this an order, not a request. This gives the impression that you are the one in control. You want to show the harasser that you are in control of the situation.

Keep in mind that confrontation is different from merely expressing your anger. The goal of confrontation is to let the aggressor know what he has done wrong and to make him stop. You might want to scream or shout obscenities. But losing your cool will not accomplish nearly as much as calmly and directly telling the harasser to stop. Aggressive behavior only invites more aggressive behavior.

Be direct. When confronting a harasser it is not necessary to worry about being polite. Avoid weak or apologetic language. Using phrases like "please," "excuse me," or "I'm sorry" makes the harasser feel in control of the situation and reinforces the idea that you are the victim. Hold the harasser accountable for his or her actions. Don't try to make excuses for them or pretend that the behavior wasn't serious. Don't back down. If someone is harassing you, it is his fault, not yours.

While it is usually best to try to say no to harassers, situations occur in which that may not be practical or possible. For instance, if the harasser is your teacher or your boss, you may be afraid that if you confront him directly he will retaliate by firing you or giving you bad grades. If that is the case, you have other means of addressing the situation, which are discussed below.

Sometimes confronting the harasser is not enough to stop the behavior. If confrontation fails, it may be necessary to complain to your school or employer, or to consider filing a lawsuit.

Taking Action in the Workplace

Sexual harassment and other forms of discrimination in the workplace are against the law. As discussed in chapter 5, Title VII of the 1964 Civil Rights Act protects employees from all forms of discrimination and harassment based on

race, religion, and sex. You can use this law to fight harassment and discrimination.

Title VII gives victims of harassment the right to sue both
their harassers and their employers for wages and other
benefits, such as promotions that were lost because of
harassment. For example, suppose you were fired or denied
a promotion because you refused your boss's sexual
advances. The court may award you lost wages, including
the money that you would have received had you won the
promotion. The court can also require the employer to
rehire or promote you.

If you experienced physical or emotional injuries, you
can ask to be reimbursed for your medical expenses.
Victims of harassment can also collect punitive damages.
These are monetary awards that are intended to punish the
harasser. Finally, the court can order your employer to stop
the harassment and to try to prevent similar problems in the
future. For instance, the court can order employers to
change or create procedures for filing harassment complaints. Companies may also be required to develop sexual
harassment education programs for their employees.

Where to Begin

If you have been a victim of harassment at work, find out if
your company has a sexual harassment policy. The EEOC
encourages companies to develop procedures for handling
complaints of harassment and discrimination. Some larger
companies even have special personnel or divisions for handling these complaints. If your workplace has a procedure for
handling harassment and discrimination complaints, start by
filing an internal complaint. In most cases this is the fastest

and least expensive way of solving the problem. Also, once you make a formal complaint, your employer can no longer claim that he or she did not know about the harassment. That way, if you decide to file a lawsuit at a later date, you will be able to prove that the company knew about the harassment.

If your company does not have a formal procedure for filing sexual harassment complaints, it might still be wise to complain to your boss or supervisor. If your boss is the harasser, complain to someone who is your boss's superior. Also keep a written record of instances of sexual harassment or discrimination. Describe what happened and who was involved.

If the Harassment Continues

If complaining to your employer does not solve the problem, you may have to file a complaint with an outside agency. In most cases, harassment and discrimination complaints are handled by the EEOC. The EEOC is responsible for enforcing Title VII for companies that have more than fifteen employees. For smaller companies there are state and local Fair Employment Practices (FEP) laws. Keep in mind: You cannot sue in court until you've filed with the EEOC.

Some people consult a lawyer before filing their complaint with the EEOC. Others wait and hire an attorney only if they end up taking their case to court. Finding and hiring a good lawyer is discussed later in this chapter.

There is a time limit for filing charges with the EEOC and FEPs; in most cases, you have only 180 days, or six months, from the last act of harassment to file your complaint. Once you file a complaint with an EEOC/FEP agency, the agency will investigate your complaint. The agency will take statements from you and your employer. They will interview witnesses and collect other evidence that the harassment or discrimination occurred. This is when your written record will prove useful. The next step is for the agency to decide there is enough evidence to determine that you were the victim of harassment or discrimination. If the agency does not believe that there is enough evidence, it will dismiss your complaint. If your case is dismissed you can still appeal or sue, but your chances of winning are not very good.

If the agency believes that there is enough evidence to determine that you were harassed, the next step is to help you settle your case. First, the agency will try to settle the case out of court. The agency will work with both you and your employer to try to reach a fair agreement. If your employer agrees to the terms you propose, then the case is settled. If not, the next step is to file a lawsuit against your employer. The EEOC can file a lawsuit on your behalf. But in most cases, you will be given a "right-to-sue letter." You can't file a lawsuit without this letter. So, if you want to go to court, you have to file a complaint with the EEOC first. It is advisable to hire a lawyer, and one familiar with sex discrimination cases, if you do take your employer to court.

EEOC and FEP agencies are required to resolve all complaints within 180 days. But most agencies have more claims than they can handle, so cases are rarely resolved that quickly. If the agency has not finished their investigation within 180 days, you can request that they give you a right-to-sue letter immediately. That way, you can move forward with your lawsuit.

Taking Action at School

Title IX prohibits sexual harassment and other forms of discrimination in school. This law applies to any school that receives federal funding, and includes most public and private schools, elementary level through college. The law holds schools responsible for allowing sexual harassment to occur, and a school found guilty of allowing sexual harassment may lose federal funding. Title IX also gives victims the right to sue for money to reimburse expenses for physical or mental injury resulting from the harassment, foreseeable future losses such as missed job opportunities, attorney fees, and punitive damages. The court can also order the school to stop the harassment, change harassment policies or develop new policies, create procedures for filing complaints, or develop training programs for employees.

In addition to Title IX, several states have laws against sex discrimination and harassment in school. Some of these state laws offer even more protection than Title IX. For example, Minnesota law requires schools to post sexual harassment policies throughout the school, to include policies in their student handbooks, and to teach students how to prevent sexual harassment and sexual assault.

Starting the Process

If you want to file a complaint, you have several options. First, you can file a complaint with your school. Title IX requires that schools develop special procedures for handling Title IX complaints. That means that most schools have procedures for handling discrimination and harassment complaints. You can also file complaints with the

Office of Civil Rights of the Department of Education. The OCR will investigate your claim. If your school is found to be guilty of allowing harassment or discrimination, the OCR will work with the school to try to remedy the situation and end the harassment or discrimination. If the school still does not comply with Title IX, the OCR can cut off its federal funding. As with Title VII complaints, you must file a complaint with the OCR within 180 days after the harassment occurs.

In addiction, victims can file their complaints directly with the court system. Unlike employment discrimination, you do not need to file a complaint with a government agency before taking your school to court.

Taking Legal Action: School or Work

If filing a complaint with your school or employer does not solve the problem, you may want to consider taking legal action. There are several advantages to filing a lawsuit. First, by suing you may receive compensation. This might include money to make up for wages you lost because of harassment, or forcing your school to reinstate a women's sports team that had been cut. You can even sue to force your employer to rehire you if you can prove you were fired because of sex discrimination.

Taking legal action may also help establish legal precedent. Once a case has been argued successfully in court, it paves the way for others to come forward with similar cases. For example, after the courts awarded damages in the case of *Franklin v. Gwinnett Public Schools*, the door was opened for other victims to sue their schools for harassment.

123

Finally, taking your harasser to court can help you know that you are doing something to fight back. Many victims find that suing their harassers improves their self-esteem and their sense of control.

There are also some disadvantages to taking legal action. First, going to court usually requires a lot of time and money. You have to find and pay a lawyer. Even after the lawyer has prepared your case, you may have to wait a long time before you can go to court.

Second, you may not win your case. Sexual harassment can be hard to prove, and it usually occurs without witnesses. The final decision often depends on whether the judge or jury believes the victim or the harasser. Sometimes the harasser blames the victim for the harassment by claiming that she dressed provocatively or encouraged the harasser in other ways. This can be very painful for the victim, who may already be blaming herself for what happened. Going to court and losing may leave a person feeling as if she has been twice victimized—first by the person who harassed or discriminated against her, and then by the court system.

Documenting Your Case

If you are considering filing a lawsuit, you can take action to improve your chances of winning in court. To build a strong case, you will need evidence of the harassment. One of the reasons the Senate Judiciary Committee dismissed Anita Hill's complaints against Clarence Thomas was that she did not provide enough evidence to prove that the harassment occurred.

You can do several things to document your case.

First, tell people about the harassment when it occurs. Talk to your friends, family, teachers, or coworkers. Find people who will listen to your complaints and take them seriously. Not only can these people give you the emotional support you need, but they will also be able to back you up if you decide to file a formal complaint against the harasser. Although it may be difficult to talk about what happened, it is best to share as many of the details as possible. It is better to say exactly what happened, and how you responded, rather than simply saying that you think you were harassed. Be sure to let people know about any physical or emotional injuries that you have suffered because of the harassment.

Another way to strengthen your case is to find other people who have been harassed by the same person. Sexual harassers are often repeat offenders. You should not assume that you are alone. You can start by asking the people that you trust at work or at school if they have had any similar experiences with the person who harassed you. If you were harassed on the job, you might also want to locate people who quit or were fired. It is possible that they left the company because of harassment.

Another way that you can document your case is to keep a diary of the harassment or discrimination. You should include the date, time, location, and a description of each episode of harassment. Give as much detail as possible. Write down exactly what happened and what you did. You should also have some proof of when the entry was written. Some people even go so far as to mail themselves the diary in a sealed envelope so that they have the postmark to show when it was written. It is also a good idea to use the kind of notebook to which sheets of paper cannot be added. That way no one can accuse you of adding things later on.

Finally, if you decide to file a formal complaint or to sue, it is a good idea to have some information about your job or academic performance. That way, if you get fired, demoted, or receive a bad grade as the result of harassment, you have some proof that it was not because of poor performance. It is illegal for your school or employer to do anything to punish you for making a harassment or discrimination complaint.

Unfortunately, it is usually up to the victim to prove that the harasser retaliated against him or her. To document your performance at work, you should save any written evaluations that you have received. If your employer does not give such evaluations, it is a good idea to get in the habit of asking for them. Save your old schoolwork, as well as papers and tests with written comments from your teacher. All of this information may prevent your harasser from retaliating against you should you decide to file a complaint.

Finding a Lawyer

One of the most important things that you will have to do if you decide to go to court is to find a good lawyer. Try to find an attorney who specializes in discrimination and harassment cases. You might start by asking friends and family for recommendations. You can also contact women's rights advocacy groups. Some of them are listed in the appendix of this book. Many organizations, such as the 9 to 5

Association of Working Women, the ACLU, and the American Bar Association, can refer you to lawyers who specialize in harassment and discrimination cases. Depending on your case, you might be able to find a lawyer who is willing to work free or at a reduced rate because he or she wants to do something to support women who have been victims of harassment or discrimination. Others will expect to be paid only if you win. But most attorneys work for hourly fees that must be paid no matter how the case turns out. If you do win your case, you may be able to recover the cost of your legal fees.

Legal issues are only one aspect of being harassed or discriminated against. There are also emotional consequences.

Finding and Giving
Emotional Support

Kenisha sat in the waiting area outside the school counselor's office, fidgeting with the zipper on her jacket. She wasn't sure why she needed to see a counselor. Now that it was all over she just wanted to forget about what happened. She felt embarrassed about the whole thing. And what if one of her friends walked by? What would they think about her needing to see a shrink? She wondered if there was a way to sneak out of the office without anyone's noticing.

Kenisha looked up as a woman called her name. "Kenisha, I'm Ms. Freedman," the woman said as she reached out to shake Kenisha's hand. Kenisha reluctantly followed Ms. Freedman into her office and sat down.

"So, what brings you here, Kenisha?" Ms. Freedman asked.

Kenisha just shook her head and stared down at her feet. "My mother wanted me to come."

"And why is that?" the counselor asked.

Kenisha explained that she had been sexually harassed by her chemistry teacher, Mr. Moore. "But I don't see why everyone's making such a big deal about it. It's over. I'm sick of talking about it," Kenisha said.

"I know that it seems like it would be easier to try to forget what happened," Ms. Freedman said. "But most people need to work through their feelings before they can move on."

Kenisha shrugged.

"Sexual harassment can bring up a lot of painful feelings," Ms. Freedman continued. "How do you feel about what happened?"

Kenisha was silent. After a long pause, she replied, "I just feel embarrassed."

"But you have nothing to be embarrassed about," Ms. Freedman said. "It wasn't your fault."

"Then why did it happen to me?" Kenisha asked.

"This could have happened to anyone. You didn't do anything wrong." Ms. Freedman paused. "Sexual harassment is never the victim's fault."

"I feel so stupid," Kenisha said as her eyes filled with tears. "Since it happened, I feel so sad. I can't concentrate on my schoolwork. I'm even having trouble sleeping." Kenisha stopped to wipe her eyes. "Is there something wrong with me?"

"No, not at all," Ms. Freedman said with a smile. "Those are perfectly normal reactions. Being the victim of harassment can be a very difficult experience."

"I just want to stop feeling this way," Kenisha said as tears streamed down her face.

"It may take some time, but I promise that you'll get through this," the counselor said in a reassuring tone. "You're a very strong young woman."

Kenisha continued to cry for a few minutes. It felt good finally to let out her feelings.

The Emotional Costs

Sexual harassment and discrimination can be emotionally devastating experiences. Victims often suffer painful feelings ranging from self-doubt to extreme anger to severe depression. All of these feelings are normal. Different people respond differently. And these feelings may change over time.

If you have been a victim of harassment or discrimination, your first reaction may be to doubt yourself. You may feel unsure whether or not you were really the victim of harassment or discrimination. You may wonder whether you simply misunderstood the situation. You may tell yourself that are just overreacting. Often it is hard to believe that discrimination and harassment really occurred. Nobody likes to feel like a victim. And it is natural to want to see the best in other people and in difficult situations. Doubting yourself is normal. But in most cases harassment and discrimination are easy to identify. If you feel that you have been a victim, pay attention to those feelings. At the very least, it might help to discuss the situation with someone you trust.

Harassment and discrimination can be difficult to talk about. If you are a victim, you may feel embarrassed and humiliated about what happened. You may worry that you did something to deserve the unfair treatment. You may wonder if you did something to encourage your teacher's sexual attention, or if you had worked harder your boss would have taken you as seriously as your coworkers. In fact, many victims are afraid to come forward because they believe that people will blame them for what happened. If you have been the victim, it is important to know that the harassment or bias was not your fault. Sexual harassment and gender bias are never the victim's fault.

Another natural reaction is anger. What happened to you was wrong and unfair. It is normal to feel frustrated and angry. You may be angry with the people who harassed or discriminated against you. You may also be angry at the people who allowed the harassment to continue. Maybe your classmates or coworkers looked the other way when you were being harassed. Maybe your friends and family did not take your complaints seriously. Often, people do not know what to say to victims of harassment and discrimination. They may tell you that you are "overly sensitive" or that you are "overreacting." They may even take the side of your harasser.

Such reactions can be very frustrating and confusing. On the one hand, you may feel angry with people for not backing you up. On the other hand, you may begin to wonder whether these people are right. Do your best to steer clear of people who cannot understand what you are going through. You need to find people who can give you the support you deserve.

It is easy to see why victims of harassment and discrimination often have difficulty trusting other people. Once someone that you've trusted has let you down, it can be very difficult to let yourself trust other people. Sometimes victims are reluctant to confide even in friends and family. But victims need to be able to share and express their feelings. Without some form of external support, they have no outlet to express their anger. As a result, this anger is often turned inward and can lead to depression. Victims begin to feel powerless and apathetic. They feel that they cannot control their own lives. As a result, many victims give up trying to fight.

Finding and Giving Support

Sexual harassment and discrimination can be difficult to discuss. Most victims need emotional support to help them recover. Victims of harassment and discrimination need to hear, "What happened to you was wrong," and "Your feelings are normal," and "It's not your fault." They need to know that they are not alone, and that thousands of women and men have been victims of harassment and discrimination. Victims need people who will help them stop blaming themselves for what happened. This support can come from friends, family, other victims, or a therapist.

If someone you know has been the victim of sexual harassment or discrimination, there are ways that you can give her the emotional support she needs. First, remind her that what happened is harassment and that it is not her fault. Even if the victim thinks that she could have done things differently, she is not at fault. Second, you should help the victim to express her anger. Many victims are reluctant or even afraid to express their anger about the harassment. They may take their anger out on close friends and family or turn it inward and become depressed. Encourage the victim to name what she is angry about and talk about it. Help her to find appropriate outlets for these feelings.

A supportive friend is someone who listens without judging. You may think that the victim should have handled the situation differently, but keep those opinions to yourself. What the victim needs is someone to listen and support her. Let her know that her feelings are normal. Even if you are having trouble understanding these feelings, never question them. Instead, affirm her feelings by making comments such as, "I know this experience was very painful for you." Perhaps the most important thing you can do is to reassure the victim that there are people who care about her, and that she will be able to get through the emotional (and possibly legal) crisis.

Keep in mind that sometimes the victim will not want to talk about her experiences. Instead, she may need someone who can help her to forget about what happened for an hour or two, just to be free of thinking about it for a while. Be sensitive to the victim's needs. Let her know that you're there if she needs you.

If you have been the victim of harassment or discrimination and are looking for support, it is important that you tell people exactly what you do and don't need. If you want advice, ask for it. If you just need to let off steam, let people know that too. Unfortunately, sometimes even the best-meaning friends may have difficulty understanding the seriousness of harassment and discrimination. Many people still have a lot to learn about the subject. They may think that it is not really a big deal, or even that it was the victim's fault (which it never is). And even if they do understand the problem, it may still be hard for some people to understand just what you are feeling. If you are afraid that a person may not offer the support you need, express your concerns (e.g., "I'm worried that if I tell you what happened you will blame me"), or confide in someone else. If at first you don't find the kind of support you need, don't give up. Keep looking until you find someone you can trust.

Sometimes talking with friends and family is not enough. Victims of harassment and discrimination may also benefit from professional therapy. Seeing a therapist does not mean that you are crazy. It is perfectly normal to need some extra help when coping with a disturbing situation or event. You may also consider joining a support group for victims of discrimination or harassment. Support groups provide a safe place where you can share your experiences with other victims.

There are many ways of finding a therapist or support group. You can ask a teacher or counselor at school. Your family doctor will be able to refer you to a professional therapist. Or you can contact an organization like the American Psychological Association or the 9 to 5 National Association of Working Women, which helps victims of sexual harassment and sex discrimination. You will find a list of these organizations at the end of this book. They can provide information about support groups in your area, as well as professional therapists who specialize in working with victims.

If you have been the victim of harassment or discrimination, you do not have to suffer alone.

Fighting Back

Sexual harassment, like other forms of gender bias, is pervasive in our society. Now that you have learned more about the issues, you know how to avoid being a perpetrator of sexual harassment and gender bias. You also know what you can do if you or someone you know is a victim. One person cannot singlehandedly stop gender bias, but you can help to reduce the problem.

Harassment and gender bias affect all of us in one way or another, and there are many things that you can do to fight back. The first step toward combating the problem is education. By reading this book you have already taken that first step. Most people do not know enough about the issues. In fact, experts believe that the majority of harassment cases could be avoided if people knew more about the matter. Education can help people avoid being harassers and help them understand the difference between harassment and flirting. When it comes to harassment and bias, many people are also confused about their rights. Education can also help the victims.

You can start at your school, where sexual harassment and gender bias may well be serious problems. Try to organize a special assembly at your school to teach students and teachers about sexual harassment. Find friends who are interested. Ask a teacher or school counselor to serve as your adviser. Some of the organizations listed at the end of this book have films and other educational materials that schools can use to teach students and faculty about sexual harassment and discrimination. These organizations may also be able to recommend experts who would be willing to give a lecture.

Another thing that you can do to fight harassment is to find out whether your school has a sexual harassment policy. As part of its fight against sexual harassment, the Office of Civil Rights requires all schools to develop harassment policies. Unfortunately, the majority of schools do not have any. Does your school have a special policy on sexual harassment or discrimination? If you are not sure, ask a teacher or administrator to help you find the answer. If your school does not have a policy, let your teacher know that you would be willing to help develop one. If your school does have a harassment or discrimination policy, ask yourself whether most students and teachers know about it. If not, you can help spread this information.

Another reason sexual harassment and discrimination are so common is that many people are afraid to speak out. There was no shortage of witnesses when female Navy officers were sexually harassed and assaulted at the 1991 Tailhook Association convention in Las Vegas. But no one did anything to stop the harassment. If you see harassment or discrimination happening, do not ignore it. Stand by the victim, or report it to someone who can help. If possible, tell the harasser to stop. If necessary, help the victim to report the incident to someone in authority.

There are ways that you can fight harassment and discrimination in your community. You can join a national women's rights organization or start a chapter in your community. Organizations like NOW are actively involved in fighting gender bias and sexual harassment. Most NOW chapters are interested in having young women join them. They may also be able to help you set up a NOW action team at your school. To find out if there is a chapter in your community, contact the national headquarters of NOW (listed at the end of this book). Check your local telephone book for listings of NOW chapters or other local women's rights organizations.

Another way that you can fight harassment and discrimination is to get politically involved by supporting candidates who are committed to equal rights for women. Although over the past few years more and more women have been elected to office, women are still a long way from being equally represented in government. Even if you are too young to vote, you can volunteer to work on campaigns.

You can start by contacting the National Woman's Political Caucus (NWPC). Their goal is to get women elected and appointed to political office. They train women on how to get elected, and teach candidates and campaign workers how to raise funds and urge people to vote. The NWPC helps women interested in serving at all levels of government, from local school boards to the White House. It also encourages young people to get involved in government by offering internships for college students. The NWPC can also give you advice about becoming a campaign volunteer.

Finally, you can feel more empowered if you take a self-defense course, many of which teach women and girls to protect themselves both physically and verbally. Developing the ability to feel comfortable and able to tell someone that he or she has crossed an inappropriate emotional or physical boundary will make you a more assertive and effective person.

Sexual harassment and gender bias are serious problems that affect everyone. These problems are symptoms of the sexist culture in which we live. Harassment and discrimination are never the victim's fault. If you or someone you know has been a victim, you do not have to sit back and take it. You deserve to be heard. Although it can be painful, you will get through the experience to be a stronger and smarter person.

Glossary

androgyny Condition of having both male and female characteristics.

chronic Long-lasting or frequently happening.

confrontation Face-to-face meeting with a challenger or an enemy.

curriculum The subjects offered by a school in a given semester or term.

discrimination Treatment of people on the basis of race, ethnicity, sex, religion, or other trait.

disparate Made up of different elements.

environment The surroundings in which one lives or works.

gender The characteristics usually associated with one or the other of the sexes.

proportionality Similarity in size or degree.

punitive Having the purpose of punishment.

socialization Adaptation of a person to the needs and demands of a society.

stereotype Prejudicial mental picture of a person or group without regard for the individual person.

vocational education Training in a skill or trade to become a life work.

Where to Go for Help

The following are major organizations and government agencies that offer information and advice about sexual harassment and sex discrimination.

American Association of University Women (AAUW)
1111 Sixteenth Street NW
Washington, DC 20036-4873
(202) 728-7602
Web site or email: http://www.aauw.org
The AAUW offers several publications on sexual harassment and gender bias in school, including *How Schools Shortchange Girls* and *Hostile Hallways: The AAUW Survey on Sexual Harassment in America's Schools.*

American Psychological Association (APA)
750 1st Street, NE
Washington, DC 20002
(202) 336-5500
Web site: http://www.apa.org
This organization provides a book on how to choose a therapist and makes referrals to professional therapists who specialize in treating victims of sexual harassment and discrimination.

Center for Research on Women
Sexual Harassment in Schools Project, Wellesley College
Wellesley, MA 02181
(781) 283-2500

The center offers educational publications on sexual harassment in schools and provides a list of other resources on
harassment at school.

Equal Employment Opportunity Commission (EEOC)
1801 L Street, NW
Washington, DC 20507
(800) 669-EEOC
(202) 634-7057 for the hearing-impaired
The EEOC handles complaints of sexual harassment and sex
discrimination in the workplace. You must file a complaint
with the EEOC before filing a lawsuit.

National Organization of Women (NOW)
Legal Defense Fund
99 Hudson Street
New York, NY 10013
212-925-6635
Web site: http://now.ldef.org
This organization provides research and referrals on a broad
range of issues affecting women and the law. NOW LDEF offers a
list of publications on sexual harassment. It also offers a
resource kit for victims of sexual harassment.

National Partnership for Women and Families
1875 Connecticut Avenue NW, Suite 710
Washington, DC 20009
(202) 986-2600
Web site: http://www.nationalpartnership.org/index.html
This national nonprofit organization provides public education
and written materials on sexual harassment.

National Resource Center for Consumers of Legal Services
6596 Main Street

Gloucester, VA 23061
(804) 693-9330
Web site: http://www.nrccls.org
email: info@nrccls.org
This center provides nationwide legal referrals to attorneys experienced in sexual harassment cases and publishes materials on how to choose a lawyer.

National Women's Political Caucus (NWPC)
271 West 125th Street
New York, NY 10027
(212) 666-0980
This national organization works to further issues of relevance to women.

9 to 5 National Association of Working Women
614 Superior Avenue NW
Cleveland, OH 44113-1387
Toll-free Job Problem Hot Line: (800) 522-0925
General Information: (216) 566-9308
Web site: http://members.aol.com/naww925
This organization offers a toll-free confidential telephone service, staffed by trained job counselors. It provides information and referrals on how to deal with sexual harassment and other problems on the job.

Woman's Sports Foundation
Eisenhower Park
East Meadow, NY 11554
(800) 227-3988 (Infoline)
(516)542-4700
Web site: http://www.lifetimetv.com/wosport
This foundation provides information and advocacy concerning Title IX and how it affects female athletes. Helps individuals

facing discrimination in school athletics programs. Offers grants to individuals and teams.

CANADIAN ORGANIZATIONS

Status of Women Canada
360 Albert Street
7th Floor
Ottawa, Ontario K1A 1C3
(613) 995-7835
Web site: webcoord@msmail.swc-cfc.gc.ca
This organization provides information concerning women and advocates equality.

Women's Center
University of Winnipeg
Room OR30
515 Portage Avenue
Winnipeg, Manitoba R3B 2E9
(204) 786-9788
Web site: http://www.uwinnipeg.ca/~uwsawc/
This center is an important resource for information concerning women's rights, equality, and sexual harassment.

For Further Reading

American Association of University Women. *Hostile Hallways: The AAUW Survey on Sexual Harassment in America's Schools.* Washington, DC: AAUW Educational Foundation, 1993 (available from the AAUW).

_____. *How Schools Shortchange Girls.* Washington, DC: AAUW Educational Foundation and the National Education Association, 1992 (available from the AAUW).

Bravo, E. and E. Cassedy. *The 9 to 5 Guide to Combating Sexual Harassment.* New York: John Wiley and Sons, Inc., 1992.

Gay, Kathlyn. *Rights and Respect: What You Need to Know About Gender Bias and Sexual Harassment.* Brookfield, CT: Milford Press, 1995.

Langelan, M. J. *Back Off: How to Confront and Stop Sexual Harassment and Harassers.* New York: Fireside, 1996.

Mazer, Norma Fox. *Out of Control.* New York: Avon, 1996.

McFarland, Rhoda. *Working Together Against Sexual Harassment.* New York: Rosen Publishing Group, Inc., 1996 .

Morris, Barbra, Jacquie Terpstra, Bob Croninger, and Eleanor Linn. "Tune in to Your Rights: A Guide for Teenagers About Turning Off Sexual Harassment." Ann Arbor, MI: Center for Sex Equity in Schools, University of Michigan, 1985 (available in English, Spanish, and Arabic from the University of Michigan; call (734) 763-9910).

Nash, Carol Rust. *Sexual Harassment: What Teens Should Know* (Issues in Focus). Springfield, NJ: Enslow Publishers, 1996.

Index

A

abilities
   doubt of girls', 12, 63
   mathematical, 20, 52–53
achievement, academic, 51–55, 64
affirmative action, 81–86
African Americans, 82–83
aggressiveness
   as male trait, 15, 20, 21, 23, 28, 36, 65
   "unsuitable" for women, 72–73
American Association of University Women (AAUW), 35, 64, 95–96
American Civil Liberties Union (ACLU), 86
androgyny, 18
anger, 117, 131,132
appearance, physical, 15, 18, 74–75, 90, 111
assault, sexual, 90, 95
athletics
   discrimination in, 5, 41
   professional, 36
athletics programs, 35–37, 42–45
   dropping, 45–49, 123

funds for, 33–35, 40, 44
attention
   to girls vs. boys, 12, 61–62
   sexual, 4, 87–89, 92, 107

B

Bakke vs. University of California, 84
basketball, 33–34, 36, 39, 42–43, 45–46, 48
behavior
   adopting stereotyped, 21–22
   "correct," 14–15
   labeling the, 117
   male/female differences in, 19–22
   naming the, 117
   sexist, 25–27
   sexual, 4, 98, 100, 104
boss
   as harasser, 6, 8, 91, 100, 106–107, 116, 118, 119
   sexist, 71–72
boys
   and sexism, 30–32, 96
   sex role pressure on, 64–67
breast cancer, 36
Bruneau, Eve, 95–96

C

careers
"female," 38, 70, 112
lower-status, 11, 38, 92
male-dominated, 12, 71, 92
male/female, 29–30
math-connected, 52
chronic harassers, 104
Civil Rights Act, 75
Clinton, Bill, 85
comments, sexual, 3, 6, 8,
73–74, 95,100,
105–106, 110
commercials, stereotyped,
28–29
complaint, filing, 120,
122–123
confrontation, 116–117
control, sense of having,
66, 117, 124, 132
Coughlin, Paula, 9
curriculum
formal, 56–60
hidden, 60–64
male vs. female, 41

D

decisions, hiring/admission,
81, 84
depression, 112, 130, 132
differences
anatomical, 25
biological, 16–17, 19–20,
52–53
within sexes, 19–20
discomfort, feeling of, 1–2, 8,
90–91, 94, 100, 108, 110

disparate impact, 79–81
disparate treatment, 78–79
Douglas, Michael, 111

E

embarrassment, feeling of, 4, 130
environment
hostile, 7, 69, 99, 100
Equal Employment
Opportunity
Commission (EEOC), 6, 8,
76, 83, 99, 120–121
Equity in Athletics Act, 45
expectations
employers', 72
parental, 23–24, 53–54

F

Fair Employment Practices
Agency (FEPA), 76, 120
favors, sexual, 4, 6, 89, 98, 100
fear
of failure, 63
of harasser, 4, 7, 118
Fennema, Elizabeth, 54
flashing, 6, 89
flirting, 90–91, 96, 102, 104,
108, 116, 117
football, 13–14, 48
*Franklin v. Gwinnett Public
Schools*, 98, 123
funding, federal, 42, 97, 122,
123

G

gender bias, 5, 7, 11–12,
13–22, 135

effects on boys, 12
and men, 102–113
at school, 33–49, 58–60,
66–67
gender identity, 24, 25
gender roles, 14–15, 23–32
as cultural ideas, 16–17
glass ceiling, 11–12
Gutek, Barbara, 107

H

Hawthorne, Nathaniel, 59
heart disease, 36
Henderson, Judge Thomas E., 86
Hill, Anita, 8–9, 91, 124
history, women missing from,
59–60
home economics, 38
homosexuality, 89, 94, 95

I

involvement, political, 137

J

Jacklin, Carol, 19, 21
jobs
lower-status for women, 38
pink-collar vs. blue-collar,
70-71
Johnson, Lyndon B., 81–83

K

Kelso, Frank III, 9

L

Langelan, Martha, 117
laws

against discrimination,
41–42, 75–76
against sexual harassment, 5,
6, 97, 99–101
lawsuit
discrimination, 47, 79–80, 86
documenting evidence for,
124–126
setting precedent, 123–124
sexual harassment, 9, 76–78,
93, 121, 123–127
lawyer, consulting, 120, 121,
124, 126–127
leadership skills, 37
Letourneau, Mary Kay, 111
literature by women, missing, 59
lookism, 73–75

M

Maccoby, Eleanor, 19, 21
Marathon, New York, 19
math, 2, 37, 50–51, 52, 53–55,
65, 66
media
message of worth in, 74–75
power of, 25–31
men
and sexual harassment, 5,
112–113
stereotypes of, 15
as victims, 109–113
Miller, Arthur, 59
minorities, opportunities for,
81–83
modeling, 24
mooning, 6, 89
Moore, Demi, 111

music videos, 27, 29
myths, cultural, 104

N

National Association of Working
    Women, 111, 126
National Council for Research
    on Women (NCRW), 10
National Organization of
    Women, (NOW), 137
National Women's Political
    Caucus (NWPC), 137
no means no, 108, 116
"no means yes," 104
nursing, 38, 70, 91

O

Office of Civil Rights (OCR), 42,
    43, 44, 97–98, 123, 136
opportunities
    denial of equal, 7, 11
    in sports, 44, 47
    for women/minorities, 81–83
osteoporosis, 36

P

Paludi, Michelle, 106
passivity, as female trait, 15,
    28, 63, 69
pay, unequal, 68–71, 76–78, 79
peer, 21
    as harasser, 6, 91, 99
peer pressure, 54–55
power
    men's, over women, 10
    as root of harassment, 90,
        104, 111

pregnancy, unwanted, 37, 42
pressure, societal, on males,
    17–18, 65–67
privileges, denial of, 7, 11
proportionality test, 43–44
Proposition 209, 85–86
punitive damages, 119, 122
putdowns, 72, 91, 96

Q

questions, personal, 3
quid pro quo, 99–100
quotas, 84

R

readers, children's, 57–58
reading, 20, 30, 51–52, 53–54
record of harassment, keeping,
    120–121
referees, women as
    professional, 36
reverse discrimination, 83–84
rewards, denial of, 7, 11
right to sue, 99, 119, 121
rights, legal, 5, 41–45, 75–76,
    97–101, 118–127
Rodgers, Bill, 19
role models, 25
    lacking for girls, 36, 39
rumors, sexual, 89, 95

S

Sadker, David and Myra, 61
school
    discrimination in, 5, 12,
        37–39, 41
    gender bias in, 33–49

harassment policies, 97
sexual harassment in, 10,
    93–94
taking action in, 122–123
science, 1–2, 37, 51, 52, 53,
    55, 66
selection, race-conscious,
    84
self-confidence, 12, 54, 66
self-defense course, 138
self-doubt, 12, 130
self-esteem
    low, 18, 54, 60
    regaining, 36, 116, 124
sex differences, 19–22, 37–38
    academic, 51–55
    biological, 52–53
sex discrimination,1–5, 7, 11,
    14, 38
    on the job, 68–86
    legalized by Prop. 209, 85
sex and gender, differences
    between, 16–17
sex hormones, 21, 52
sexism, 13–22
    in school materials, 56–58
sex objects, women as, 28, 75,
    94 104, 107
sexual harassment, 1–5,
    87–101
    adult-student, 95, 97, 98, 99,
        102
    costs of, 94–96
        emotional, 130–132
    defined, 6–12
    male/female views of,
        106–108

and men, 102–113
"reasonable woman"
    standard for, 107–108
rules for avoiding, 108
student-student, 97, 98–99,
    102
Shakespeare, William, 59
Sherman, Julia, 54
socialization
    boys', 65–66, 104
    male/female, 21–22, 63–64,
        69
social work, 70
sports
    contact, 36, 42
    financial assistance for, 42–44
    girls discouraged from, 23
    as male domain, 35–36
    revenue from, 43, 46, 48
    school budgets for, 40–41
    value of, 36–37
Steinbeck, John, 59
stereotypes
    gender, 15–18, 24, 53, 62, 63
    male/female, 5, 51–55
    sex-role, 21–22, 24–25, 27,
        53–54, 112
    costs of, 30–32
    in textbooks, 57–58
stranger, as harasser, 6, 90, 91,
    116
Strug, Kerri, 14
substance abuse, 37, 66
suicide, 66, 95
support, emotional
    finding, 128, 132–134
    giving, 132–133

support group, 134
Supreme Court, U.S., 84, 86,
    98, 99

T

Tailhook Association, 9, 136
teacher
    as harasser, 1–4, 6, 91, 99,
        100, 118, 128–130
    interaction of students with,
        61–63
television and children, 27–28
tests, standardized, 20, 37–38,
    52
textbooks, sexist, 56–59, 60
therapy, professional, 134
Thomas, Clarence, 8–10,
    124
Title VII, Equal Pay Act (EPA),
    76, 78–80, 82, 99–101,
    118–119, 123
Title IX, Educational
    Amendments of 1972,
    42–44, 47–49, 97–99,
    122–123
touching, unwanted, 6, 89, 95
toys, stereotypes in, 21, 29
treatment, girls/boys, 23–24, 37
truancy, 1, 96
trust, loss of, 131–132

U

Ugarte, Tianna, 95

V

verbal skills, as female trait,
    19–20
visual-spatial ability, as male
    trait, 20
vocational education, 38, 41

W

Waitz, Grete, 19
women
    in Congress, 11–12
    opportunities for, 81–83
    in school curricula, 58–60
    stereotypes of, 15
    on television, 27, 29–30
Women's National Basketball
    Association (WNBA), 36
women's studies, 59–60
workforce, women in, 11,
    70–71
workplace
    rights in, 99–101
    sex discrimination in, 68–86
    sexual harassment in, 10–11,
        91–93
    taking action in, 118–121
writing, 51–52, 64

Y

Year of the Woman, 11–12